ROYAL MARINES
APPLIED
PHYSICAL TRAINING
HANDBOOK
1945

INCLUDING
BAYONET FIGHTING
AND
CLOSE COMBAT

21936

The Naval & Military Press Ltd

Published by

The Naval & Military Press Ltd

Unit 5 Riverside, Brambleside,
Bellbrook Industrial Estate,
Uckfield, East Sussex,
TN22 1QQ England

Tel: +44 (0) 1825 749494
Fax: +44 (0) 1825 765701

www.naval–military–press.com
www.nmarchive.com

ROYAL
ARMOURIES

The Library & Archives Department at the
Royal Armouries Museum, Leeds, specialises
in the history and development of armour
and weapons from earliest times to the
present day. Material relating to the
development of artillery and modern
fortifications is held at the Royal
Armouries Museum, Fort Nelson.

For further information contact:
Royal Armouries Museum, Library, Armouries Drive, Leeds, West Yorkshire LS10 1LT
Royal Armouries, Library, Fort Nelson, Down End Road, Fareham PO17 6AN

Or visit the Museum's website at
www.armouries.org.uk

ADMIRALTY.

December 1944.

The **Applied** Physical Training Handbook, Royal Marines, 1945, is promulgated for the guidance of Officers and N.C.O.'s, more particularly for those not qualified in P. & R.T. duties.

I desire to emphasize to all the extreme importance of fitness. There is no task, whether strenuous or sedentary, that cannot be carried out more efficiently if mentally and physically fit.

Lieutenant General,

General Officer Commanding,
Royal Marines.

1—21936

DAILY EXERCISES

1. The object is to keep all men agile, active and young. To ensure that the greatest benefit is obtained it is essential that these exercises should be carried out every day and not spasmodically.

The exercises have been compiled and grouped in a simple manner so that they can be taught easily by both Officers and N.C. Officers who are not qualified as P.T. Instructors.

2. The exercises are divided into eight groups and classified under the following headings :—

> (1) Loosening.
> (2) Chest.
> (3) Trunk I.
> (4) Trunk II.
> (5) March and Run.
> (6) R.T. Games.
> (7) Jumping.
> (8) Corrective.

Groups Nos. 1—4 and 8 contain four exercises, each having the same physical effect, and are of approximately equal strength.

The object of each group is as follows :—

(1) *Loosening*.—To stimulate the circulation of the blood and to loosen the shoulder, hip, knee and ankle joints.

(2) *Chest*.—To work the muscles of the chest and back and to ensure free breathing.

(3) *Trunk I*.—To exercise the lateral muscles of the waist and to assist digestion.

(4) *Trunk II*.—To exercise the frontal muscles of the stomach, assist the digestion and carriage of the body.

(5) *March and Run*.—To assist correct carriage of the body and improve circulation and breathing.

(6) *R.T. Games*.—To encourage competition and team spirit and to exercise the whole body.

(7) *Jumping*.—To teach control, courage, lightness, judgment of distance and agility.

(8) *Corrective*.—To maintain the correct carriage of the body.

CONDUCT OF EXERCISES

Table

1. Normally only one exercise from each group should make a table. Time taken for one table of exercises should be approximately seven to nine minutes.

If more time is available two or more exercises from each group should be done, in fact, the number of exercises performed depends on the time available.

2. It is essential that the instructor should be able to teach all the exercises in each group.

To encourage keenness and maintain interest, full use should be made of the different exercises in each group. A typical table would be as follows :—

Number 2 exercise from Number 1 group.

,, 1 ,, ,, ,, 2 ,,
,, 3 ,, ,, ,, 3 ,,
,, 4 ,, ,, ,, 4 ,,

Marching and Running for about one minute.

R.T. Games for about two minutes.

Jumping for about one minute.

Number 3 exercise from Number 8 group.

Instructors

1. The Instructor should ensure that sufficient space is available for the performance of various exercises.

To avoid waste of time by opening a class by drill movements, classes should be opened by :—

(1) Using the command—" Open out in front of me—Go."

(2) Spot or team method as used in the gymnasium.

2. The Instructor must always place himself in a position where he can be seen by the whole class.

3. Until a class has a good knowledge of the exercises, the Instructor should first demonstrate, then take each exercise by numbers.

4. When the class have a good knowledge they may be done judging the time, when the executive word will be " Commence." The Instructor should always work with the class when possible.

5. The Instructor should ensure free breathing at all times throughout the table.

6. *The Instructor must always work out his table beforehand and know it thoroughly before taking a class.* (*See* para. 2.)

7. Particular care should be taken that no pause or dead point occurs between one exercise and the next.

8. Surprise and order movements should be inserted at any time to keep the class mentally alert. (*See* page 20.)

Clothing

If time is available it is suggested that shorts and shoes be worn, but at any time it is essential that tunics, caps and braces be removed, and in warm weather shirts and flannels also.

4

LOOSENING GROUP

Starting Position	Exercise
1. STANDING	Astride jump with— 1. Arm raising sideway. 2. Arm raising sideway and forward. 3. Hand clapping over head and behind back.
2. STANDING	Skip jump with arms stretching. 1. Sideway. 2. Upward. 3. Sideway, upward, sideway and downward.
3. STANDING	Skip jump with feet placing forward and backward. 1. With hip firm. 2. With opposite arm swinging upward and backward. 3. With hand clapping over head and behind back.
4. STANDING	1. Hopping on alternate feet with leg swinging sideway. 2. Hopping on alternate feet with leg swinging sideway with opposite arm swinging upward.

NOTE.—The order " Steady " will be given to finish all the above

LOOSENING GROUP

Caution	Executive W.O.C.	Necessary Caution

Astride jump with——
  1. Arm raising sideway
  2. Arm raising sideway and forward
  3. Hand clapping over head and behind the back
	COMMENCE	Keep class in time by counting.

Skip jump with arm stretching——
  1. Sideway
  2. Upward
  3. Sideway, upward, sideway and downward
	COMMENCE	Keep class in time by counting.

1. Hips—— Skip jump with feet placing forward and backward 2. With opposite arm swinging upward and backward 3. With hand clapping over the head and behind the back	FIRM COMMENCE	Keep class in time by counting.
Hips—— Hopping on alternate feet with leg swinging sideway to the left—— Hopping on alternate feet with leg swinging sideway and opposite arm swinging upward to the left with the right arm——	FIRM COMMENCE COMMENCE	Toe pointed, body upright.

exercises, the class will then return to the Starting Position.

TRUNK GROUP I (LATERAL)

Starting Position	Exercise
1. STANDING WIDE ASTRIDE, ARMS SIDE-WAY	1. Keeping the arms in line with the shoulders, bend down and touch the toe with the opposite hand, looking towards the upper hand. 2. Return to the Starting Position. 3. Repeat exercise the opposite way. 4. Return to Starting Position.
2. SITTING—LEGS APART and STRAIGHT, ARMS SIDEWAY.	1. Twist the trunk to the left and touch opposite toe with hand. 2. Return to Starting Position. 3. Repeat the other way. 4. Return to Starting Position.
3. STANDING WIDE ASTRIDE, ARMS UP-WARD, HANDS CLASPED	1. Circle the trunk sideway and down-ward to the left. 2. Repeat to the right.
4. STANDING WIDE ASTRIDE, ARMS SIDE-WAY, FISTS CLENCHED	1. Twist the trunk to the left. 2. Bend down and touch ground with the right fist between the feet. 3. Resume position one. 4. Resume Starting Position.

TRUNK GROUP I (LATERAL)

Caution	Executive W.O.C.	Necessary Caution
With a jump, feet wide astride and arms sideway—— Touch alternate toe with opposite hand to the left and right by numbers——	RAISE ... 1—2—3—4	Look towards upper hand, legs straight.
Sitting with legs apart, and arms sideway position—— Trunk twisting with toe touching to the left and right by numbers——	READY ... 1—2—3—4	Back straight. Look round at other hand.
With a jump, feet wide astride and hands clasped above the head—— Trunk circling to the left (right)—— Class——	READY COMMENCE STEADY ...	Stretch up with the arms. Circles with arms to be as large as possible. Head between arms
With a jump, feet wide astride and arms sideway, with fists clenched——. Trunk twisting and bending to the left by numbers—— Repeat to the right by numbers——	READY 1—2—3—4 1—2—3—4	(2) Look towards upper hand. Legs straight.

TRUNK GROUP II (ABDOMINAL)

Starting Position	Exercise
1. FRONT SUPPORT ...	1. Feet placing forward and backward quickly. 2. Bend the arms, keeping the body stiff. 3. Bend the arms and raise first the left leg, then the right.
2. KNEELING, KNEES APART	Hands on hips, trunk lowering backward. This exercise can be made harder by placing the arms in the upward bend or upward stretch position.
3. SITTING	Hips firm—bend the knees up as far as possible. This exercise can be made harder by placing the arms in the upward bend or upward stretch position.
4. LYING ON BACK ...	1. Raise and lower the legs. 2. Raise the legs and part them. 3. Raise the legs—part them—then legs circling.

TRUNK GROUP II (ABDOMINAL)

Caution	Executive W.O.C.	Necessary Caution
Front Support—— Feet jumping forward and back by numbers—— Arms—— Arms bending with alternate leg raising. Left and right by numbers—— Stand——	PLACE ... 1—2 BEND— STRETCH 1—2—3—4 UP	Hands wider than shoulders, fingers inclined inwards. Look up, stomach up, seat down.
Kneeling astride—— Hips—— Trunk backward—— Trunk upward—— Stand——	PLACE ... FIRM LOWER RAISE UP	Draw chin in and fall back from the knees, keep body in straight line.
Sitting position—— Hips—— Knee bending quickly by numbers—— Stand——	READY ... FIRM ... 1—2 UP	Body upright, back hollow.
Lying on back—— Legs raising by numbers—— Legs halfway—— Legs parting—— Legs—— Legs halfway—— Legs apart—— Legs circling outward—— Legs together and to the ground— Stand——	READY ... 1—2 RAISE 1—2 ... LOWER RAISE PLACE COMMENCE LOWER UP	Hands into the sides. Don't hold breath. Point toes. Lower the legs quietly.

MARCHING AND RUNNING

Exercise	Caution
MARCHING	Quick——
RUNNING	Double——
KNEE RAISING	With knee raising——
LEG RAISING	With leg raising——
RAPID MARCHING	Rapid marching——
MARCHING ON TOES... ...	On the toes——
HOPPING ON ALTERNATE FEET WITH LEG STRETCHING BACKWARD — HIPS FIRM	Commencing with the left foot (or right), taking the hip firm position——

NOTE.—In these marches the Executive word of command " March" the order is " Quick March "—given as the left foot reaches the ground.

MARCHING AND RUNNING

Executive W.O.C.	Necessary Caution
MARCH	Fingers straight. Chins in.
MARCH	Run on toes.
MARCH ...	Toe pointed in front of knee. Thigh parallel to ground.
MARCH ...	Leg straight, toe pointed. Keep rear heel on ground.
COMMENCE ...	Heel and toe.
MARCH	Stretch up at each step.
HOP	Lift up. Rear leg straight.

or " Hop " is given on the left foot, and to get the class marching again

RECREATIONAL GAMES

(No Gear Required)

Game	Notes
Relays, Various— 1. Running ... 2. Hopping ... 3. Medley ...	About 25 yards each way. Hop one way on one foot, back on the other. No. 1 runs, No. 2 hops, No. 3 hare jump, No. 4 runs backwards, etc.
Over to You ...	Form class in a circle sitting on ground, feet touching. One man stands in centre, and keeping his body absolutely stiff from head to heel, falls over. Men sitting down try to push him around circle. The man who allows him to touch the ground takes his place.
Tank Tracks ...	Teams line up in single file, feet wide astride, and bending down grasp one hand of the man behind them through their legs. Starting from the rear each man in turn lies down on his back, placing his seat near the head of the man in front of him, moving back to do so. The grasp must be maintained. When this is complete, the team regain their places from rear to front, taking care not to break the grasp.
Out Scouts ...	Teams line up in single file, sitting down. Number teams from front to rear. Instructor calls a number, the men in teams with that number run to a given point and back to their place.

RECREATIONAL GAMES—*continued*

(No Gear Required)

Game	Notes
Bumping Sides ...	Make a large circle on the ground. Two teams in circle with a distinguishing mark. Hands are placed behind back. Each team tries to bump the other out of the circle.
O'Grady ...	Too well known to require description.
Wrestling on Horseback	Teams line up about 15 yards apart. Any number may take part. Teams divide up into horses and jockeys and on a signal charge towards each other and try to pull their opponents off their horses.
Message Carrying Relay	Stand one man about 10 yards away from team. Give him a message to memorize. On a signal No. 1 runs to him and takes the message and on a signal from him No. 2 runs up and does likewise until the message has been passed to all the team. The last man shouts aloud the message he has received.
Loop the Loop ...	Line teams up in single file. Draw a circle about 2 feet in diameter on the floor with a mark in the centre. No. 1 stands on the edge of circle and bends down with his eyes fixed on the centre point. On the word "go" he spins around the circle 10 times, keeping his eyes on the centre mark and then runs to a given point about 15 yards away and back, then touches No. 2, who repeats this, and so on throughout the team.

JUMPING GROUP

Starting Position	Exercise
STANDING	Bend the knees and jump as high as possible into the air, landing with the knees bent, then come to the position of attention.
STANDING	Upward jump, turning right or left or about. Act as in 1 above and turn in the required direction in the air.
LEAP FROG	Line men up in single file.
BROAD JUMP FORWARD	1. Raise on toes and arms forward. 2. Bend knees, body forward—arms back. 3. Jump forward—using arms to assist. 4. Land on toes—knees bent. 5. Resume position of attention.
GROUND WORK	Forward and backward rolls and cartwheels may be carried out if mats are available or on suitable grassland.

NOTE.—If time and dress allows, and box horse is available, it should

JUMPING GROUP

Caution	Executive W.O.C.	Necessary Caution
Upward jump——	GO ...	Toes pointed, body erect.
Upward jump and turn (right), (left) or (about)——	GO ...	Turn the head sharply.
No. 1 for Leap Frog—— (At which leader takes three paces forward and makes ready)——	READY ... In stream GO	Each man takes up position three paces after completing jump.
Broad jump forward, with strong arm swinging——	GO ...	Get as far forward as possible.
—	—	—

always be used, provided the Instructor is capable of saving properly.

CORRECTIVE GROUP

Starting Position	Exercise
1. STANDING, ARMS FORWARD BEND	Arms in the forward bend position, fists clenched (*i.e.*, right fist over left elbow, left fist under right elbow). (1) Force the elbows back. (2) Return to Starting Position. (3) Fling arms sideway. (4) Return to Starting Position.
2. STANDING WITH ARMS ACROSS BEND	1. Arms in the across bend position (*i.e.*, arms in line with shoulders and bent at the elbows with the fingers straight. The fingers nearly touching chest). (1) Bend the knees and fling the arms sideway. (2) Resume Starting Position.
3. STANDING	1. Raise on the toes and raise arms sideway. 2. Bend the knees and raise the arms upward. 3. Resume Position 1. 4. Resume Starting Position.
4. STANDING WIDE ASTRIDE WITH THE ARMS PLACED BACKWARD	1. Bend the body forward as far as possible, keeping the back hollow and at the same time swing the arms upward vigorously. 2. Resume Starting Position.

CORRECTIVE GROUP

Caution	Executive W.O.C.	Necessary Caution
Arms forward—— Elbow and arm flinging by numbers—— Arms downward——	BEND ... 1—2—3—4 STRETCH	Keep the arms in line with the shoulders. Head still.
Arms across—— Knee bending with arm flinging by numbers—— Arms downward——	BEND ... 1—2 STRETCH	Keep arms in line with shoulders. Elbows back.
Heels raise and arms sideway—— Knee bending and arms raising upward. By numbers—— Heels sink and arms downward——	RAISE ... 1—2 LOWER	Fingers stretched. Turn the knees outward.
With a jump, feet wide astride and arms backward—— Trunk bending forward with arms swinging upward by numbers—— Class——	PLACE ... 1—2 'TION	Body well forward, get the arms in line with the ears. Chin in.

SURPRISE MOVEMENTS

1. Sit down.
2. Touch four walls.
3. Bombs falling.   (Lie down.)
4. Face E., N., S., W.
5. Face some particular spot or building.
6. Touch wood, or brass, metal rope, leather, canvas or other object.
7. Touch right heel with left hand.
8. Left arm upward bend, right hand, hips firm—arms change (one movement).
9. Odd numbers sit down—ranks change.
10. Odd numbers around even numbers, even around odd.
11. Odd numbered ranks around even numbered ranks—even around odd.
12. Gas ! } See what class will do ! !
13. Fire !
14. Off the floor—go.
15. On the left (or right) knee—kneel.
16. Men whose names begin with (name a letter) sit down.
17. Men whose names contain 3, 4, 5, 6, 7, 8, etc., letters sit down. (Men sit down as the number is called which affects them.)

NOTE.—Many others may be introduced.

P.E.—TABLE " A "

INTROS.	...	Surprise movements and livening-up Exs.
		(St.) Hd. bend. b.
		(St.-Asd.-Hp. Fm.) Tr. bend. f. and d.
		(St.-Asd.) Tr. bend. s. w. opp. Am. bend. ur.
LG. I.	...	(St.-Hl. Ra.-U. Bd.) Kn. bend. w. Am. stretch u. (1—2).

SPAN.	...	(St.-Asd.-Hn. Bhd. Th.) Hd. press. b. (1—2).
SUPPL.	...	(St.) Touch Toes.

HV.	...	(St.) Am. stretch, in 4 directions.
BAL.	...	(St.-Asd.-Hp. Fm.) Alt. Kn. rais. (1—4).

DOR.	...	(St.-Asd.-Rvs. Am. S.-Tr. F.) Am. rais. u. (1—2).
ABD.	...	(Fr. Sup.-Asd.) Alt. Am. rais. f. (1—4).
LAT.	...	(St.-Asd. Am. S.-Clen.) Tr. turn. quickly (1—4).

MCH. and RUN.	Mch. 1 minute (140 paces to minute).
	Run 2 minutes or two relay races.
	Mch. w. Kn. rais.
BR.	(St.) Am. rais. s. (3).

LEAP	...	U. Jump. U. Jump. and turn. all directions.
		Leap frog.
		Skip jumps. Various.
		Thro' V. (::) or. 2 backs. in stream.
		Asd. V. (::) or. 2 backs. in stream.

FIN.	...	(St.) Hd. turn. quickly (1—4).
		(St.-Am. S.) Paces f.w. Am. fling.
BR.	...	(St.) Hn. turn. o. and in. (3).

TABLE " B "

INTROS. ...	Surprise movements and livening-up Exs.
	(St.) Hd. circl.
	(St.-Asd. U. Bd.-Clen.) Alt. Am. punch. f. w. Tr. and Hd. turn. (1—4).
	(St.-Asd.-Hp. Fm.-Tr. F.) Tr. circl.
LG. I. ...	(St.-Kn. Fl. Bd.-Hp. Fm.) Hop. 3 on spot.

SPAN. ...	(St.-Asd.-Am. B.-Clasp.) Ct. lift. w. Hd. press. b.
	or
	(Pn. Ly.-Am. B.-Clasp.) Ct. lift. w. Hd. press. b. (1—2).
SUPPL. ...	(Crh.) Lg. straighten. (1—2).

HV. ...	(St.-Am. F.-Butcher's Hook Gr.) Am. punch. and pull w. resist. (:) (in 2 ranks).
BAL. ...	(St.-Ft. F.-Hl. Ra.-Am. S.) Quick Kn. bend. and slow stretch. (1—2).

DOR. ...	(St.-Asd.) Tr. bend. f. w. Am. swing. u. (1—2).
ABD. ...	(Fr. Sup.) Am. bend. (1—2).
LAT. ...	(St.-Wd. Asd.-Am. S.-Clen.) Tr. turn. and bend. to touch ground between Ft. (1—4).

MCH. and RUN.	Mch. 1 minute. (150 paces to minute).
	Rapid marching and sprinting alt.
	Obstacle relay.
	Mch. w. Lg. rais.
BR. ...	(St.-Am. F.) Hl. rais. w. Am. part. (3).

LEAP. ...	Revise all U. jumps.
	Thro' V. (::) or. 2 backs.
	Asd. V. (::) or. 2 backs.
	Asd. V. (::) or. 3 backs. T. shape.
	Star jump. Repeat jump from land. (3).

FIN. ...	(St.) Hd. circl.
	(St.-U. Bd.) Am. stretch. u. (1—2).
BR. ...	(St.) Am. rais. s. w. Hl. rais. (3).

TABLE " C "

INTROS.	...	Surprise movements and livening-up Exs. (St.) Hd. turn. quickly. (1—4). (St.-Asd.-Am. S.) Alt. Toe touch. w. opp. Hn. (1—4). (St.-Am. F.) Kick Hn. 3 times w. each Ft.
LG. I.	...	(St.-Kn. Bd.-Hp. Fm.) Kn. bend. to sit and stretch, ½ way quickly (1—2).

SPAN.	...	(St.-Asd.-U. Bd.) Ct. lift. w. Hd. press b. (1—2).
SUPPL.	...	(St.-Asd.-Am. U.) Tr. swing. d. and u. (1—2).

HV.	...	(St.) Am. stretch. in 4 directions.
BAL.	...	(St.-Kn. Ra.-Hp. Fm.) Lg. stretch. f.

DOR.	...	(St.-Asd.-Rvs. Am. S.-Tr. F.) Am. circl. (small circles slowly).
ABD.	...	(Fr. Sup.). Am. bend. w. alt. Lg. rais.
LAT.	...	(St.-Wd. Asd.-Am. U.) Tr. bend. s.w. same Kn. bend.

MCH. and		Run 3 minutes.
RUN.	...	Mch. 1 minute. (160 paces to the minute).
LG. II.	...	(St.-Kn. Fl. Bd.) Rst. Am. ac. Th.

LEAP.	...	Hurdle Relay Race (:) Class in single file, Kn. fl. bd. 1 Am. s. Revise all V. in Tables " A " and " B ". Add (St.-Hp. Fm.) Skip jump w. Ft. plac. f. and b.

FIN.	...	(St.-Am. F.) Hl. rais. w. Am. part. (1—2). (St.) Hd. bend. b. and f. (St.) Touch Toes.
BR.	...	(St.) (3).

TABLE " D "

INTROS. ...	Surprise movements and livening-up Exs.
	(St.-Hd. B.-Ac. Bd.) Am. fling.
	(St.-Asd.) Alt. Ak. grasp. (1—4).
	(St.-Asd.-Ac. Bd.) Tr. turn. quickly w. Am. fling. (1—4).
R.T. GAME	Relay race. Fireman's lift.

| SPAN. ... | (St.-Asd.-Hn. on Ct.-Clen.) Ct. lift. w. Am. part and Hd. press. b. |
| SUPPL. ... | (St.-Wd. Asd.-Ak. Gr.) Walk Ft. tog. keeping Lg. straight. |

| HV. ... | (B. Hg.) Am. bend. w. alt. Lg. rais. (::) (in single rank or circl.). |
| BAL. ... | (St.-1. Lg. F.-Am. F.) Am. and Lg. carry. s. (1—2). |

DOR. ...	(Hz. Sit.-U. Bd.) Am. stretch. u. and pull. d. w. resistance (:) Sup. gr. In Butcher's Hook and r. Lg. sup. centre of Bk.
ABD. ...	(Bk. Ly.) Lg. rais. and part. (1—4).
LAT. ...	(St.-Wd. Asd.) Am. U. Clasp. Tr. circl. .

| MCH. and | Run 3 minutes. |
| RUN. | Mch. w. Kn. rais. and Lg. rais. |

LEAP. ...	Thro' V. or. 2 backs (::).
	F. Roll. B. Roll. Hn. St. (:). Cartwheel.
	Stick jump relay.

FIN. ...	(St.-Am. S.) Hd. turn. quickly w. Hn. turn. u. and d· (1—4).
	(St.-F. Bd.) El. and Am. fling. (1—3).
BR. ...	(St.) (3).

This table is specially designed for use indoors or a dry field.

APPLIED PHYSICAL TRAINING

" Applied " Physical Training means various forms of physical exercises which are not carried out in a gymnasium but are specially applied to the training of men for active service.

It is an established fact that if some form of apparatus is used the individual, both separately and in mass, is more interested in the work than if free standing exercises, or P.E. as it is known, are carried out. " Applied " P.T. has therefore been introduced to meet this demand and also to increase the strength of ordinary P.E.

Another asset of this form of P.T. is that the laggard who does not want to work has a fair chance of getting away with it in ordinary P.E., whereas in Applied P.T. the apparatus used makes him work, and the exercises have been devised to this end.

The general aims and methods of Physical and Recreational Training in the R.M. are not always sufficiently understood. It should be appreciated by all officers, N.C.Os. and marines that the role of the Corps requires particular attention to the aspect of fitness of all ranks to a high degree, and it is emphasized that a personal interest must be taken by everyone to achieve and maintain the required standard.

The underlying psychological reasons for this training may here be explained. The main principle is contained in the old adage " mens sana in corpore sano," which literally translated means " a healthy mind in a healthy body," but there is much more to it than that.

If the average man is physically fit his mind is also in much better trim, because the ordinary functions of the body are working smoothly, and no mental effort is required to overcome anything in the nature of strain like liver disorder, constipation, etc. Thus the fit man feels better and happier, whereas the unfit man much more easily develops a " grouch " or " moan " which is often without real foundation.

In other words, a fit man looks on the bright side and an unfit man on the dismal side of life.

In the first instance, the recruit undergoes a basic course of physical training in the gymnasium under qualified instructors to build up his physique and improve his mental alertness in order to make him fit enough to tackle advanced training in all subjects. This is carried out in Group I training and is based on Handbook of P. and R.T., Volume I.

Following this course Applied P.T. is carried out as laid down by G.O.C. R.M. in the Recruit Training Syllabus, culminating in the passing of Physical Efficiency Tests.

In order to maintain the required standard of physical fitness, all ranks will be exercised in all forms of Applied P.T. during their service, and revision squads and pre-embarkation training will include the passing of the physical efficiency tests. N.C.Os. will pass these tests after their promotion course. (This will be noted on the drill history sheet (P.P.E.T.) on every occasion.)

The basic P.T. course being carried out in the gymnasium is done in P.T. kit, but the object of Applied P.T. is that it should be done in progressive stages of clothing and equipment so that the culminating physical efficiency tests are carried out in full battle order.

Due care should be taken with regard to the hygiene of this training, but it must be appreciated that the encumberment of equipment and rifle makes the scaling of obstacles very much harder and of more practical value than when carried out in P.T. kit, and must be practised.

It is further pointed out that whilst a number of P.T. Instructors are available to teach and train men in these various forms of exercises, it is well within the power of Officers and N.C. Officers who are not specialized in P.T. to train their own units on these lines.

In many temporary bases or camps where operational units have to be maintained in a high state of physical fitness and where no gymnasium is available, simple outdoor apparatus can be erected. Details of this are shown in diagrams under their appropriate heading.

The various forms of exercise. are as follows :—
1. Rifle exercises.
2. Log exercises.
3. Tubular bar work.
4. Balance work.
5. Rope work.
6. Tug-o'-war.

The objects of each group of exercises are briefly as follows :—

1. **Rifle Exercises.**—Strong exercises to develop forearms, biceps, back and shoulder muscles. They also give a man confidence and ability in the handling of his primary offensive weapon.

2. **Log Exercises.**—These exercises are designed to produce a similar effect to rifle exercises ; at the same time teaching the value of teamwork.

3. **Tubular Bar Work.**—Development of the heaving and abdominal muscles, also, to teach men the preliminaries to clearing obstacles.

4. **Balance Work.**—To teach men to negotiate high obstacles, and generally to accustom them to moving on narrow surfaces at heights such as lower booms in ships.

5. **Rope Work.**—The practical application of climbing vertical and horizontal ropes, such as climbing a rope from sea level to deck of a ship or traversing a stream or street.

6. **Tug-o'-War.**—To teach men teamwork and the art of heaving on a rope, so that this can be applied in a practical manner in boatwork, repository, etc.

RIFLE EXERCISES

These exercises have been formulated to provide a table which is more strenuous than an ordinary free standing P.E. Table.

They are particularly suitable in conditions where no apparatus whatever is available as in a ship or temporary camp.

The majority of these exercises can be performed with the aid of the band to assist in keeping the time, an alternative method being for the Instructor and class to whistle or sing a popular tune.

A table consists of one or more exercises from each group of
    Loosening
    Chest
    Abdominal
    Lateral
    Game
    Corrective.

If space is available a short sharp run preferably with rifle at the trail should be inserted after lateral exercises.

In a normal period of 12 minutes two exercises from each group should be taken, each exercise being repeated four times, allowing two minutes for running.

Conduct of Exercises

1. The class should be opened out as for P.E., care being taken that there is sufficient room between men.

2. The rifle is grasped at the small of the butt and at the band, muzzle to left, magazine downwards.

3. Orders to be given : Position ready.
                          Exercise commence.
                          Steady.

4. Exercise to be repeated few or many times according to the state of training of the troops.

5. Care must be taken that when rifle is in upward stretch position the upper arm is not in front of ear and the chin well in.

6. Don't forget to insert the small arm aiming exercise occasionally.

7. Some of these exercises can be done on the march, movement of rifle being with every third pace.

8. The instructor must do the exercise himself with a rifle in order to get the correct timing. The tendency is to go too fast.

9. The timing and rhythm of all exercises varies with the effort required.

10. Most of these exercises must first be done by numbers to ensure that the class performs the movements correctly. When they are understood the exercises should be done judging the time.

Loosening Group

Starting position   *Exercise*   *Caution*

1. Standing feet astride, arms upward.

Rifle circling.

Keep rifle at full arm's length throughout, and when overhead as vertical as possible.

2. Knees full bend, hands wide apart on rifle resting on knees.

Jump upwards, rifle over the head, legs apart, and return to land in starting position.

Movement of legs as in Star Jump.

Loosening Group—*continued*

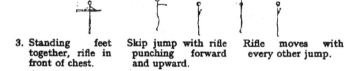

3. Standing feet together, rifle in front of chest.

Skip jump with rifle punching forward and upward.

Rifle moves with every other jump.

4. Standing, rifle on thigh.

Skip jump with foot placing forward and backward with rifle swinging forward and upward.

Rifle moves with every jump.

Chest Group

Starting position	*Exercise*	*Caution*

1. Standing feet astride, rifle on thigh.

1. Bend the arms.
2. Stretch arms upwards.
3. Bend arms and place rifle behind head.
4. Press head back.
5. Stretch rifle upward.
6. Swing down to place rifle on insteps and press twice.
7. Return to S.P.

Tuck head well in and keep legs straight in position (5).

2. Standing, feet astride, rifle on thigh.

1. Swing rifle upwards and press twice.
2. Swing down to place rifle on ground and press twice.
3. Swing to position (1) and press twice.
4. Return to S.P.

Keep head back and stomach in position (1). Legs straight and head in on 2nd movement.

3a—21936

Chest Group—*continued*

Starting position	*Exercise*	*Caution*

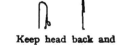

3. Standing, feet astride, rifle on thigh.

1. Bend the trunk forward and swing arms upwards.
2. Bend arms and place rifle behind head.
3. Press head back.
4. Stretch arms upward keeping trunk forward.
5. Bend down and beat floor three times.
6. Return to S.P.

Keep head back and force chest forward in position (3).

4. Kneel on one knee, rifle rested on knee.

1. Swing rifle upward, look up to rifle and press twice.
2. Swing rifle forward and downward reaching as far forward as possible and press twice.
3. Swing to position (1).
4. Return to S.P.

Keep head back in position (1). In position (2) turn forward foot out and force the chest to the knee.

Trunk (I) Lateral

Starting position	*Exercise*	*Caution*

1. Standing, feet astride, grasping the rifle in both hands above the head.

1. Bend the trunk sideway.
2. Press twice.
3. Return to S.P.

Bend the trunk directly to the side and not forward or backward.

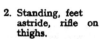

2. Standing, feet astride, rifle on thighs.

1. Turn trunk sideways and swing arms upwards.
2. Press once.
3. Return to S.P.
4. Repeat (1) to opposite side.
(Progress 1–2 rhythm).

Raise on rear heel when in sideway position. Look up at rifle.

Trunk (I) Lateral—*continued*

Starting position	*Exercise*	*Caution*

3 Standing, feet astride, right arm forward grasping the rifle, muzzle vertical.

1. Twist the body to the right.
2. Swing round to the left as far as possible.
3. Return to position (1).
4. Return to S.P.
Change hands and repeat to other side.

Do not check the body when in the twist position.

4. Standing, feet astride.

1. Turn trunk to place the butt between the feet in rear.
2. Return to S.P.

Exercise to be done slowly, keeping feet flat on the ground.

Trunk II (Abdominal)

Starting position	*Exercise*	*Caution*

1. Standing, feet together, arms forward. Rifle parallel to ground.

Knee raising to kick shoulder with the knee inside the rifle.

Keep body upright and steady.

2. Standing, feet together, arms forward, rifle parallel to ground.

Leg raising to kick rifle with instep.

Keep body steady and leg straight.

3. Lying on the back with rifle behind the shoulders. Ankles supported by opposite rank.

Trunk raising vertical and lower slowly.

Back straight, head back.

Trunk II (Abdominal)—*continued*

Starting position	*Exercise*	*Caution*

4. Lying on the back, rifle on the insteps. Rifle resting on the feet. Feet slightly apart. Arms upward.

Leg raising (about 6 ins. off the ground).

Flatten the back and breathe normally.

CORRECTIVE GROUP

Starting position	*Exercise*	*Caution*

1. Standing rifle across thighs.

   1. Raise rifle and leg forward.
   2. Carry leg to rear and swing rifle above head.
   3. Carry leg forward and lower rifle to forward position.
   4. Return to position of attention.
Repeat with other leg.

Keep head back in position (2). Keep toe pointed in all leg movements.

2. Standing rifle across thighs.

   1. Place left foot forward and raise rifle forward.
   2. Turn on heels to the right and swing rifle upward.
   3. Turn on heels to the front and return to position (1).
   4. Return to S.P.
Repeat with right foot.

A short pace forward only should be taken in position (1).

Corrective Group—*continued*

| *Starting position* | *Exercise* | *Caution* |

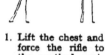

3. Standing feet astride, grasping the rifle behind the back, rifle resting against the back. Magazine to the rear.

1. Lift the chest and force the rifle to the vertical position.
2. Return to S.P.

The position of the arms to be adjusted on the rifle according to man's height so that arms are straight.

4. Knees slightly bent, rifle forward.

1. Swing rifle upward and fully bend the knees.
2. Return to S.P.

This exercise should be done quickly.

NOTE.—In taking these exercises note particularly Conduct of Exercises, para. 10.

RECREATIONAL GAMES

1. Weight carrying relay

On the order " Go " the leader will collect all the rifles of his team, run to a given point, return and hand the rifles over to No. 2, and so on throughout the team. Rifles should be carried in the crook of both arms in front of the chest or slung over each arm. To finish the game each man will collect his own rifle from the last man to run and stand to attention.

2. Jumping Relay (1 rifle only required)

On the order " Go " the leader will run to a given point and back with the rifle. No. 2 will grasp the other end of the rifle and they will run through the team with the rifle about 1 ft. from the ground, the remainder of the team jumping over the rifle. No. 2 then repeats with No. 3 and so on throughout the team.

3. Under and Over

As for Rifle Jumping Relay, except the rifle is passed over the head of the first man, the second man jumps over the rifle and so on throughout the team. Men should be spaced about 1 yd. apart.

4. Rifle Wrestling in Pairs

Men stand 1 yd. apart and hold the rifle with one hand near the point of balance and one at muzzle or butt. The object is to gain complete possession of the rifle. Feet should not be moved more than is essential.

Many other similar games can be played.

NOTE.—The greatest care must be taken when playing these games that rifles are not dropped or damaged in any way.

LOG EXERCISES

The objects of these exercises are :—

1. To develop the art of teamwork.

2. Particularly to develop heaving and trunk muscles and to co-ordinate movements of the legs and arms.

A convenient sized log is about 18–21 ft. long, 6–8 ins. in diameter and about 200–250 lb. in weight. A team for a log of this size should be 8 to 10 men, depending, of course, on the general physical ability of the team. The aim is to get all men of equal height in one team, in order that every man carries his proportion of the weight of the log. If this is impossible teams should be sized. This is a most important aspect of the work. If logs of this description are not available it will be seen that many of the exercises can be carried out with spars, capstan bars, stanchions, etc.

These exercises are split up into the following groups :—

1. Heave.
2. Trunk I (Lateral).
3. Trunk II (Abdominal).
4. Games.
5. Leg and Arm.

Each group consists of exercises which are all quite strenuous, and therefore not more than two exercises should be selected from each group for one lesson, making a total of ten exercises.

Conduct of Exercises

These exercises should be conducted in a similar manner to P.E· The starting position should be adopted and the exercises carried out either by numbers or by giving the orders " Commence " and " Steady." It is most important that all men move smartly on the executive word of command ; otherwise the exercises will be badly done and half the benefit lost.

HEAVE GROUP

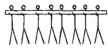

1. Standing feet astride, log on one shoulder.   Arm stretching upward and bending to place log on opposite shoulder.

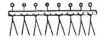

2. Standing feet astride, log in crook of both arms.   Log passing sideway.   In this exercise, as the end man of team loses the log he runs to the other end of team to his new position and so on throughout the team.

3. Circle formation about 3 ft. apart.   One end of log to centre of circle, other end of log held by one of the team.
   Pass log round the circle quickly.

4. Feet astride, log held above the head, arms straight.
   Log passing forward and backward.   End man on losing the log runs to other end of team and so on.

LATERAL GROUP

1. Standing astride, log under one arm.

Trunk bending sideway away from log with opposite hand reaching downward.

2. Feet astride, log under one arm.

Trunk bending sideway towards log with opposite arm swinging upward.

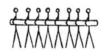

3. Feet astride, log on shoulder.

Trunk bending sideway with opposite arm reaching downward.
(Slight bend only.)

4. Feet astride, log on ground by right feet.

Trunk bending sideway to pick up log and swing overhead to place on the ground by left feet. Repeat exercise to other side.

ABDOMINAL GROUP

1. Sitting on the ground, on alternate sides, of the log, log in crook of arms. Trunk bending forward and backward.

2. Standing, log in crook of arms, one hand over-grasp, the other under-grasp.

  1. Bend forward to reach toes with log.

  2. Raise log above the head so that it is supported on the palms of the hands.

  3. Return to starting position.

3. Feet astride, log in crook of arms.

Log lower to thighs and throw high to opposite team.

4. Lying on the ground, log in crook of arms. Trunk raising to reach the toes with the log.

LOG GAMES

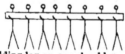

1. Feet astride, holding log on one shoulder. Run with log to given point (up to 80 yds.). Team race.

2. Feet astride, log between legs. Galley race about 20 yds.

3. Feet astride, holding log between legs. Quick passing foward and backward. The man on the end of team on losing the log runs to other end of team and so on.

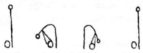

4. All the team stand on right of the log. On the order " Go " they lift the log over the head and place on the ground on their right, then jump over the log so that once again they are on the right of it. This is repeated a given number of times.

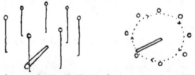

5. The team form a large circle so that one end of the log is at the centre of the circle. On the order " Go " the leader picks up the outer end of the log and runs clockwise round the circle with the log and then hands it to the man on his original left.

This is repeated throughout the team.

LEG AND ARM GROUP

1. Standing feet astride, log on one shoulder. Knee bending and stretching.

2. Feet astride, log held above the head, arms straight. Knee bending and stretching with arms bending and stretching to place log on opposite shoulder.

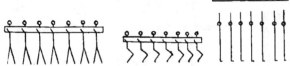

3. Feet astride, log on shoulder. Knee bending and stretching with vertical high throw, catching log and placing it on opposite shoulder.

4. Feet astride, log on ground on right side. Trunk bending sideway to pick up log and place on right shoulder, and knee bending and stretching to throw log vertically and catch to place on left shoulder with knee bending. Repeat to other side.

TUBULAR BAR WORK

1. The diagram below shows a simple structure of tubular scaffolding, which can be erected with R.M. labour, for use in bases or camps where no gymnasium is available.

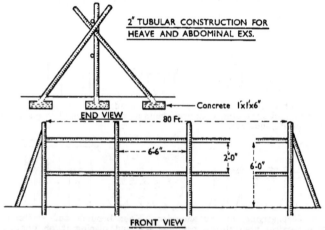

2" TUBULAR CONSTRUCTION FOR HEAVE AND ABDOMINAL EXS.

2. The exercises on this apparatus are divided into five groups :—
    Heave.
    Dorsal.
    Abdominal.
    Lateral.
    Obstacle clearing.

3. Care must be taken that this form of training is progressive and not overdone. Some of these exercises are very strong—hence until the general service officer or N.C.O. in charge has some experience of them, they should only be taken by a qualified P. and R.T. Instructor.

4. The exercises should at first be carried out in loose order, but later in fighting order so that the men become accustomed to performing strenuous tasks in this dress for obvious reasons.

TUBULAR BAR WORK

Heave Group

Starting position	Exercise	Caution
1. (B. Hg.)... ...	Am. bend. Progress to :— Am. bend. w. alt. Lg. rais. (1–4).	Chin in. Body in one straight line from Hl. to Ak.
2. (Sit. Lower Bar.-Or. Hv. Gr.)	Am. bend. to (Sit.-Hv. Hg.) to lift seat off lower bar. Progress to :— Lg. stretch. f. and part.	Chin in, elbows back, Chest out.
3. (Sit.-Lower Bar.-Ur. Gr.)	Circl. to (Bal. Sup.-Top Bar).	Bend Ams. first and let Hd. go back. (Teach progressively if required).
4. (Fr. Knl.-Or. Gr.-Top Bar).	Am. bend. Progress to :— Am. bend. and Kn. part.	Adjust position of Ams. according to height of man.

Dorsal Group

Starting position	Exercise	Caution
1. (Fr. St.-Asd.-Tr. F.-F. Gr.-Lower Bar).	Tr. press. d. Progress to :— Tr. press. d. (:)	Keep Ams. straight, Chin in, Bk. hollow. Support place one Hn. on upper part of Bk. and assist the pressing.
2. (Hi. Pn. Ly.-Fxd.-Lower Bar-Rvs. Am. S.).	Am. circle. b. (:)	(:) at ankles. Upper thigh over bar.
3. (Fr. St.-F. Gr.-Top Bar).	Ct. press. d. w. alt. Lg. swing. b.	Look up. Keep Ams. and Lg. straight, toe pointed.
4. (Fr. St. Asd.-F. Gr. Lower Bar.-Tr. F.-Hd. ur. Bar).	Hd. press. b.	Distance between ft. to be adjusted according to height of men. Force Hd. back to get Nk. against bar.

Lateral Group

Starting position	Exercise	Caution
1. (Fr. St.-Asd.-Tr. F.-F. Gr. Lower Bar).	Alt. Ak. Gr. and opp. Am. swing u. (1–8).	Look up at Am. Keep Am. grasping the bar straight.
2. (St.-Asd.-Bk. to Bar).	Tr. turn. to gr. upper and lower bar (1–4).	Hd. to assist turn of Tr. to the left—left Am. lower bar, right Am. upper bar.
3. Sd. St.-Lg. Ra.-Fxd.-M. Gr.).	Lower Lg. rais. (1–2) (:)	Keep Hips up. Support holds upper leg.
4. (Hi. Asd. Sit.-Fxd.-Ac. Bd.-Top Bar).	Tr. turn. w. Am. fling (1–4).	Lock the feet under lower bar.

Abdominal Group

Starting position	Exercise	Caution
1. (B. Angle Hg.-Top Bar).	Kn. rais. Progress to :— (i) Kn. rais. and part. (ii) Lg. rais. (iii) Lg. rais. and part.	Do not hold the breath. Hands wide apart.
2. (Low. Fr. Sup.-Lower Bar).	Am. bend. and stretch.	Seat up. Body in a straight line from toes to head.
3. (Hi. Sit.-Fxd.-Top Bar-Hp. Fm.).	Tr. lower b. Progress to :— (i) Tr. lower b. to parallel w. ground. (ii) Tr. lower b. w. Am. stretch. u.	Ft. hooked lower bar. Ct. to lead movement when returning to S.P.
4. (Hi. Sit. in Hocks Am. U.-Fxd.-Top Bar).	Tr. lower b. to touch ground w. Hns. and regain S.P. on bar (:)	Ft. are held by support. Ex. to be done as slowly as possible.

Obstacle Clearing Group

1. Obl. Hv. V. (1 pace).
2. Gate V.—1 Ft. on Lower Bar.
3. 2 Hn. Sd. V.—1 Ft. on Top Bar.
4. (Sit.-Elbows on Top Bar). Press to Bal. Sup.

BALANCE WORK

There is more in Balance Work than would at first appear. A high degree of mental and physical co-ordination, courage and judgment are required which can only be gained by constant practice. Few men are not perturbed at working at heights on narrow platforms ; this is mainly due to inexperience. Contempt is bred by familiarity ; therefore to overcome any difficulty practice is the answer.

Careful progression is required to build up a man's confidence. Most ranks have carried out balance exercises in the gymnasium in their early training, and the same principles are now applied to a more natural obstacle.

All exercises are first to be carried out in loose order, progressing to fighting order with rifle.

The rifle should be carried in the Port Arms position but somewhat away from the body, and used to asist in the balance by moving as necessary in the counter-balance movements.

Exercises should be carried out first on the ground, then on low, followed by high apparatus (*see* diagrams).

1. Ground

(*a*) *Ghost Walk.*—Used for silent approach by night (in long grass or undergrowth). Raise the arms forward and somewhat upward where they are in a convenient position to feel obstructions, and can assist in the general counter-balance movements. The foot is raised off the ground to about the knee raising position and placed silently on the ground, taking a fairly short pace, the whole of the flat of the foot to meet the ground at the same time. Gradually transfer the weight of the body on to this foot and then when steady continue this at every pace. If suddenly illuminated by Verey light or starshell, momentarily remain perfectly still and then slowly freeze to ground level. When caught in a difficult position a good sense of balance is essential, and this can only be gained by constant practice.

(*b*) *Listeners* v. *Stalkers* (by day and night).—Place one unit in a defensive position and use another to approach. This can be practised in the day, by blindfolding the defending side, or by night. Various forms of competitions can be arranged to make this an interesting form of training.

2. Low apparatus

    (*a*) Marching forward.

    (*b*) Marching sideway.

    (*c*) Knee raising.

    (*d*) Crawl (rifle slung).

    (*e*) Speed tests.

    (*f*) Nerve tests (throw thunder flashes, smoke in vicinity).

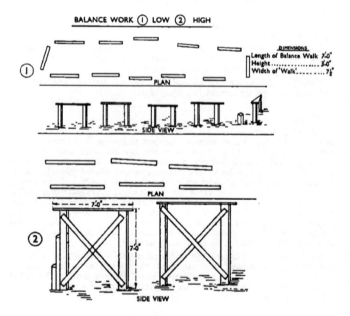

BALANCE WORK ① LOW ② HIGH

DIMENSIONS
Length of Balance Walk 7'0"
Height .... 3'0"
Width of 'Walk' .... 7½"

3. High apparatus

Repeat above lessons.

Games may be arranged to increase confidence such as team *v.* team, *e.g.*, balance march forward, return under the apparatus zigzagging around uprights.

Useful Hints in How to Balance

1. Look carefully at obstacle before starting.

2. When balance actually starts DON'T look down but keep eyes directed at own height fixed on an object.

3. Before moving forward transfer weight of body on the foremost leg by outward movement of the hip.

4. Counter-balance movements, *i.e.*, movements of body arms and knees to maintain balance, should be done smoothly and *not* with a jerk.

5. If balance is being lost bend knees outwards and get as low as possible, later slowly straightening to regain position.

6. If balance is lost completely during training, ensure that the landing is made with knees bent to avoid injury.

ROPEWORK

The ability of the Marine to climb a vertical rope and traverse a horizontal rope is of paramount importance both from a soldiering and seafaring point of view. To be successful the correct and easiest methods must be mastered, in order to avoid undue fatigue.

The elementary method of climbing a vertical rope has been taught to all ranks in their initial P.T. course in the gym, in gym kit.

The following exercises should be taught and carried out in boots (loose order), progressing to fighting order, rifle slung.

1. Climb vertical rope *(see* diagram)

Note the first motion is the most important part of this climb particular attention being paid to the grip of the feet.

2. Make fast vertical rope (*see* diagram)

The object of this position is to enable a man to have both hands free for some other purpose and still maintain his position on the rope.

Climb to the required height, part the legs, pass the right leg outside and around the rope so that this is twisted around the leg and resting across the instep. Clamp the rope with the sole of the other foot on to the instep, then pass the right arm in front of the rope forcing it to the rear by forcing the chest forward.

3. Horizontal rope (cat crawl) (*see* diagram)

This is useful in crossing rivers, chasms, tops of houses and other obstacles where no other more convenient method exists.

Lie out centrally along the top of the rope, hands well forward, allowing one leg to hang loosely downwards and at right angles to the rope. The other leg should be well bent and knee turned outwards, instep over rope. To move along the rope, pull with each hand alternately with a firm and steady movement.

To regain position on rope, if balance is lost

The right hock should be cocked over the rope, left leg left hanging. The hands gripping the rope should be placed right hand above chest, left hand above neck with elbow cocked over rope. Then with a swing of left leg and pressing on left elbow, position can be regained on top of the rope.

Pendulum Swing.—For short distances, the pendulum swing is advisable (*see* diagram)

This method means hanging supported by hands only and swinging the body like a pendulum, shifting each hand alternately in the required direction with the swing of the body.

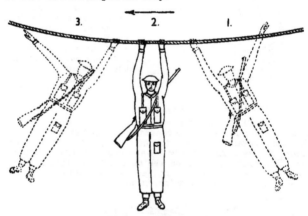

PENDULUM SWING

TUG-O'-WAR

This has been included in applied physical training syllabus, because it is an interesting way to teach men how to use their muscles and weight in pulling on a rope, and how to pull as a team.

The practical applications of pulling on a rope are many and various both from a seafaring and soldiering point of view, such as pulling a vessel alongside when power is not available, hoisting boats, dragging a vehicle, gun or tank out of a bogged position to assist or in lieu of mechanical means.

There is also the psychological factor in tug of war practice which is valuable from a training point of view. The principles brought out in this training are that a successful team have got to display the ability to :—

1. Immediately react to an order and all together as one man.

2. Hang on to the last ounce of endurance.

3. All serve equally as a team.

4. Realize that nothing really good can be achieved without assiduous training.

This is not a treatise on tug of war as carried out in the Olympia competition, but merely a few useful hints for the uninitiated. Of first importance is the

Position on the rope

Body at a comfortable angle. Side of the inner foot and heel of the outer foot on the ground, legs apart, knees slightly bent for quick movement. Body and legs almost in line, foremost arm straight, hands together, shoulder over rope, head well up and looking towards your opponents. Men can pull on either side of the rope, whichever suits them better.

To Heave

Lower the rope and body slightly, push backwards with the full force of both legs, allowing the arm and the body to conform to the movement. Stand by to obtain a fresh grip with the feet and retain the ground gained. Remember not to move feet until you have got to, and then the team should move as one man.

To Check

Used to break a heave or stop the weight from taking charge. From this position prepare to heave again.

A Live Rope

To do nothing is to do something definitely wrong on a rope. Once the rope becomes still it is easy for an opposing team who are lively to take the initiative, and this must be prevented.

Footwork

Don't move your feet until you've got to, then move together and dig in (*see* Heave). If you do you are liable to lose perhaps a good foothold and never gain another. The feet when moved should be carried out quickly and dug in hard so that pressure from the legs may be immediately applied.

Rhythm of the Pull

A well trained team can feel just what to do and when to heave, check, move their feet, by acquiring rope sense and team work. This of course can only be acquired by plenty of training and good coaching.

OUTDOOR TUBULAR GYM

This apparatus is designed as an outdoor gymnasium, and most exercises which are done in a fully equipped indoor gymnasium can be performed on this structure.

It is particularly suitable for fleet bases, rehabilitation centres and camps where an indoor gymnasium is not available.

Fig. I shows the complete structure and Fig. II is a plan of the apparatus.

A list of the gear required to rig this apparatus is as follows :—

(a) Gymnasium

20 ft. lengths	...	...	47
18 ft. lengths	...	...	20
16 ft. lengths	...	...	35
Tubular joints	...	...	232
Swivel joints	...	...	16

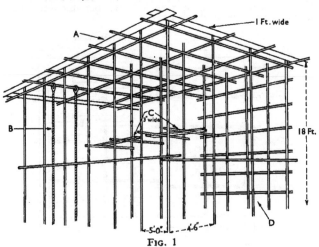

FIG. 1

(b) *Additional for Window Ladders* (marked " D " on Fig. I)

20 ft. lengths	...	...	...	...	...	8
10 ft. lengths	...	...	...	...	...	28
9 ft. lengths	...	...	...	...	...	13
Tubular joints	...	...	...	...	...	78
Swivel joints	...	...	...	...	...	2
Extension joints		...	...	...	...	6

The following additional points should be noted :—

1. Weights for tug-o'-war practice can be conveniently erected in the centre of the structure.

2. High balance or confidence walk can be rigged around the top of apparatus (width 1 ft., marked A on Fig. I).

3. Tubular bar exercises *(see* p. 46) can also be carried out on the window ladder side of the apparatus.

Four tables are included in this book which should be taken by a qualified P.T. instructor where one is born. These tables have the advantage that they can be done in boots, but this instruction is dependent naturally on the weather.

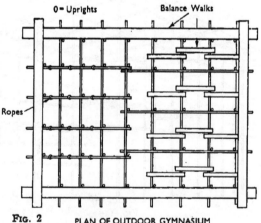

FIG. 2   PLAN OF OUTDOOR GYMNASIUM

TUBULAR TABLE 1

Group	Exercise	Progression	Remarks
INTROS. ...	Livening-up Exs.		
	(St.) Hd. circl.		
	(St.-Asd.-U. Bd.-Clen.) Alt. Am. punch. f. w. Tr. and Hd. turn. (1—4).		
	(St.-Asd.-Hp. Fm.-Tr. F.) Tr. circl.		
LG. I. ...	(St.-Kn. Fl. Bd.-Hp. Fm.) Hop. 3 on Spot.		

SPAN. ...	(St.-Asd.-Am. B.-Clasp.) Ct. lift. w. Hd. press. b.		
SUPPL. ...	(Crh.) Kn. straighten.		

HV. ...	(Hg.-Or. Gr.) Am. bend.		
LAT. ...	(St.-Asd.-Between Bars.) Tr. turn. to gr. low as possible (1—4).		
ABD. ...	(Hg.) Kn. rais.	Lg. rais.	
DOR. ...	(Fr. St.-Or. Gr.) Alt. Lg. stretch. b. (1—4) (½ class top of W. L.-Am. U. in S.P.)		

HV. II. ...	(Climb and Make Fast.-continue straight to Bal. Exs.		
BAL. ...	(Bal. Mch. F.)		

MCH. and	150'—Rapid Mch. and Sprint. Alt.-Mch. w. Lg. rais.		
RUN.	1 min. Obstacle Relay.		
BR. EXS....	(St.-Am. F.) Hl. rais. w. Am. part.		

LEAP. ...	Revise all U. Jumps.	Thro. V. (::) Or. 2 Backs.	
		Asd. V. (::) Or. 2 Backs.	
		Asd. V. (::) Or. 3 Backs. T. Box.	
		Star Jump. (3)	

FIN. EXS.	(St.) Hd. circl.		
	(St.-U. Bd.) Am. stretch. u. (1—2)		
BR. EXS....	(St.) Am. rais. s. w. Hl. rais. (3)		

TUBULAR TABLE 2

Group	Exercise	Progression	Remarks
INTROS. ...	Livening-up Exs.		
	(St.) Hd. turn. quickly (1—4)		
	(St.-Asd.-Am. S.) Alt. Toe touch. w. opp. Hn. (1—4)		
	(St.-Am. F.) Kick Hn. 3 times w. each Ft.		
LG. I. ...	(St.-Kn. Bd.-Hp. Fm.) Kn. bend. to sit. and stretch. ½ way quickly (1—2)		
SPAN. ...	(St.-Asd.-U. Bd.) Hd. press. b. w. Ct. lift. (1—2)		
SUPPL. ...	(St.-Asd.-Am. U.) Tr. swing. d. and u. (1—2)		
HV. ...	(Obl. Hg.-Or. Gr.) Am. bend.	All class face 1 way.-1 pace right close. Odd teams left incline, even teams right incline.-Odd teams Dor. even teams Hv.	
DOR. ...	(Obl. St.-In. Gr.) Alt. Lg. stretch. b.		
ABD. ...	(Obl. Hg.) Kn. rais. and part. (1—4)		
LAT. ...	(Obl. St.-Asd.-Bk. to 1 Bar.)	Tr. turn. quickly to gr. in line w. waist. Odd teams face side of bars. Even teams face end of bars. Class 1 pace left close mch. Bk. to your own bar. ½ pace F. Mch.	
HV. II. ...	(Climb Tubular Upright.-on completion commence Bal. Exs.)		
BAL. ...	(Bal. Mch. F. w. Kn. rais.)		
MCH. and RUN.	Run 3 min. Mch. 1 min. (160 paces).		
LG. II. BR. EX.	(St.-Kn. Fl. Bd.-Am. Rst. Ac. Th.)		
LEAP. ...	Hurdle Relay Race. (:) Class in single file Kn. Fl. Bd.-1. Am. S.		
	Revise vaults in Table 1. Add.-(St.-Hp. Fm.) Skip. jump w. Ft. plac. f. and b.		
FIN. EXS.	(St.-Am. F.) Hl. rais. w. Am. part.		
	(St.) Hd. bend. b. and f.		
	(St.) Touch Toes.		
BR. EXS.	(St.) (3)		

TUBULAR TABLE 3

Group	Exercise	Progression	Remarks
INTROS. ...	Livening-up Exs.		
	(St.-Ac. Bd.-Hd. B.) Am. fling.		
	(St.-Asd.) Alt. Ak. grasp. (1—4)		
	(St.-Asd.-Ac. Bd.) Tr. turn. quickly w. Am. fling. (1—4)		
R.T. GAME	Relay Race. Fireman's Lift.		
SPAN. ...	(St.-Asd.-Hn. on Ct.-Clen.) Ct. lift. w. Am. part. and Hd. press. b.		
SUPPL. ...	(St.-Wd. Asd. Ak. Gr.) Ft. move together w. straight Lg.		
HV. ...	(Hv. Hg.-Or. Gr.) Alt. Am. walk. s. Am. jump. s.		
LAT. ...	(Knl.-Asd.-In front of Bars.-Bk. to Bars.) Tr. turn. quickly to gr. in line w. Ct.		
ABD. ...	(Hg.) Insteps to the Bar (1—2)		
DOR. ...	(St.-Asd.-F. Gr. Tr. F.) Tr. press. d.	½ in 5th. W. L.-Gr. in line w. Ct.	
HV. II. ...	Climb 1 rope.-cross tubular.-down 2nd rope.- continue with Bal.		
BAL. ...	Bal. Mch. F. w. Kn. rais. Lg. rais.		
MCH. and RUN.	Run 3 min. Mch. w. Kn. rais. Mch. w. Lg. rais.		
LEAP. ...	Thro. V. Or. 2 Backs. (:) F. Roll.-B. Roll.-Hn. St. (:) Cartwheel. Stick Jump Relay.		
FIN. EXS.	(St.-Am. S.) Hd. turn. quickly w. Hn. turn. u. and d. (1—4)		
	(St.-F. Bd.) El. and Am. fling. (1—3)		
BR. EXS....	(St.) (3)		

TUBULAR TABLE 4

Group	Exercise	Progression	Remarks
INTROS. ...	Livening-up Exs.		
	(St.-Asd.-Forearm. Hz.-Gr. Rifle at P. of Bal.) Am. stretch (1) and Tr. turn. w. Am. swing. s. (2) and Am. bend. and stretch. (3—4) Return swing. f. (5) Return to S.P. (6)-Repeat other side.		
	(St.-Asd.-Rifle on Th.) Lg. swing. f. and b. w. Am. swing. f. and u. (1—8)		
	(St.-Asd.-Rifle on Th.) Tr. bend. f. w. Am. swing. u. (1—2)		
LG. I. ...	(St.-Butt on Toe.-Hn. on Muzzle.) Lg. rais. (3)		
SPAN. ...	(St.-Asd.-Rifle on Th.) Am. bend. and stretch. u. and bend. to place Rifle bhd. Sh. blades. (1—8)		
SUPPL. ...	(St.-Asd.-Rifle on Th.) Am. swing. u. and Tr. bend. d. to place Rifle on Insteps.		
HV. ...	(Hi. Sit.-Am. U.-Ur. Gr.) Am. bend.	½ squad top W.L.	
DOR. ...	(Hi. Sit.-Fxd.-Am. F.-Clen.-Tr. ½ B.) Am. swing. u. and f. quickly.	W.L.	
ABD. ...	(Hi. Sit.-Fxd.-Hp. Fm.) Tr. lower. b. Tr. Hz.	W.L.	
LAT. ...	(Knl. Asd.-Hd. Rst.) Tr. bend. s. and press. and Tr. turn. to gr. Bar in line w. Ct.		
HV. II. ...	(Hi. St.-U. Gr.) Alt. Am. walk. u.	1. Rope.-1. Tubular.	
BAL. ...	(Bal. Mch. S.)	continue from Hv. II.	
MCH. and	Mch. w. Am. punch. u. (Rifle) Am. punch. f.		
RUN.	Monkey Run Relay. Relays Various.		
LG. II. ...	(St.-Rifle on Thigh.) Kn. bend. w. Am. rais. f.		
LEAPING	Revise and Add.-Nk. Roll. (::) 2 Backs. Hurdle Thro. V. (::) 2 Backs.		
	Skip Jumps Various.		
FIN. EXS.	(St.-Asd.-Rifle on Th.) Tr. turn. w. Am. swing. u.		
BR. EXS....	(St.) (3)		

PHYSICAL EFFICIENCY TESTS

The following P.E. Tests have been designed after careful consideration and experience with large numbers of men.

It is as easy and necessary to develop pride of achievement in physical training as it is in marksmanship.

It has been found that by setting these standards men have developed a keen sense to achieve them and consequently the whole physical tone of the mass has been vastly improved.

Mental alertness, speed of movement and endurance, combined with an efficient use of weapons is aimed at.

These tests are not merely to train a recruit up to a peak standard on completion of Group II training and thereafter allow him to fend for himself, but periodically to make the trained marine conscious of his duty in the maintenance of physical fitness in peace and war.

During Group I training the basic course of Swedish P.T. is completed and a *qualification is awarded*. On completion of Group II training the following tests are carried out, and noted passed or failed on the Drill History Sheet "*P.P.E.T.*/18.11.45. They are further carried out during pre-embarkation training and revision classes, and by Officers and N.C.O.'s in promotion classes ; in this latter case they are a requisite to pass the course.

It will be seen therefore that Commanding Officers will, on perusal of the D.H.S., have an immediate check on the physical capabilities of their men, and further that the men themselves will have at all times something to aim at in the taking of their exercise. Most important, these tests will have the effect of bringing to notice the importance of the maintenance of the standard of physical fitness required in all ranks at all times.

Group I

1. 10 *miles march*. 2¼ hours. Fire 5 rounds. Three hits must be scored. ·22 snap target at 30 yds.

2. *Crawl*. Leopard crawl 45 yds. in 1 minute. Pitch two out of three 36 grenades into a 10 ft. circle at 20 yds. range.

3. *Run* 2 *miles* on roads—18 minutes.

64

Group II
- 4. *Vertical rope.* Climb 18 ft.
- 5. *Horizontal rope.* 15 ft. above ground. Cat crawl 40 ft.
- 6. *6 ft. high wall.* With a run clear without assistance.

Group III
- 7. *Broad jump.* Clear ditch 9 ft. wide.
- 8. *Fireman's lift.* Carry fully equipped man and his rifle 100 yds. in 45 seconds.
- 9. *Balance walk.* 5 ins. wide at 7 ft. height. Without falling off walk four lengths of 8 ft. each, 2 ft. gaps between lengths which are slightly staggered.

Dress.—All tests will be carried out in Battle Order with 50 rounds of ammunition, rifle and steel helmet, water bottles three-quarters full.

To obtain a " Pass," a candidate must pass two out of three tests in each group.

STANDARD SWIMMING TEST

60 yds. equipped in fighting order with boots on, rifle and 50 rounds ; life belt inflated ; in sea. In fresh water 30 yds. only.

NOTE.—The swimming belt should be worn just above the belt of the equipment and secured thereto. The tape usually worn round the neck should be between the legs. Equipment should be weighted to 28 lbs. in all not including steel helmet and rifle.

BAYONET FIGHTING—ROYAL MARINES

This Section is intended to be a reminder for P. & R. T. Instructors and a text book for Officers and N.C.Os. on Bayonet Fighting in the Corps.

SYSTEM OF TRAINING

The system of Bayonet Fighting taught in the Royal Marines is generally designed to fit a man to act promptly in " action " in whatever circumstances he may find himself.

In order to produce this result in a trained man it is essential that in initial training a certain amount of drill movements must be carried out to attain ease of handling, and confidence in his weapon. When fully trained, men should be exercised frequently so that their initial training is not forgotten.

The use of the " Ring and Blob Stick " is the best method of obtaining this automatic action, *but* it must be skilfully and intelligently handled.

The *ferocious* aspect of the training and the inculcation of the fighting spirit must be very thoroughly emphasized and carried out otherwise the training will fail in its effective value.

There are two main Principles to be applied in Bayonet Fighting. They are :—

(1) Always keep the initiative, i.e., attack first. If taken at a disadvantage, make a Parry preparatory to renewing the attack.

(2) Retain your tactical advantage by maintaining your most advantageous distance from your opponent, i.e., whenever you have a chance, return to the " On Guard " position so that you can use the Long Point in preference to the shorter ones and thereby engage your enemy as far away from your own body as possible.

METHOD OF INSTRUCTION

Progression

The progression of all instruction will work up in the phases :—

(i) At the Halt—i.e., Stationary.

(ii) At the Quick—i.e., advancing one or more paces.

(iii) At the Double or Charge.

These phases of instruction will be carried out :—

   (i) In Class formation. *See* Appendix I.

  (ii) By Ring and Blob Stick. *See* Appendix II.

 (iii) On Bayonet and Obstacle Course (including Bullet Work). *See* Appendix III.

EXPLANATIONS

It is essential that every Instructor should know exactly the reason for everything taught.

If men are told why it is necessary to do something they should remember it, but if they are merely ordered to do it without a reason they are more likely to make the same mistake repeatedly.

Bayonet Fighting is all logical, and a good Instructor should use the time while the men are resting to explain " why."

POSITIONS

The High Port

When moving in close order, or in the final assault with bayonet fixed, the rifle should always be carried in this position (until the final order to charge).

The rifle is raised in front of the body with the left hand in line with the left eye, the magazine to the front, the right hand remaining as in " On Guard " position (*see* next paragraph).

This is the best position to avoid accidents in practice and in action.

On Guard

This is the position from which the Long Point is carried out and should always be assumed when in close contact with the enemy.

The Grip.—The rifle is gripped with the right hand below the small of the butt with two fingers on either side of the notch and the left hand just above the band.

If the hand grips the small of the butt, which is more comfortable, and the rifle is cocked, the right thumb will be badly cut by the cocking piece when " withdrawing." Left hand. If the fingers are inside the sling it is impossible to slide the hand forward as required when withdrawing or delivering a Short Point.

The Stance.—The left foot should be forward and the feet separated as if one had stopped in the act of walking forward, the left knee slightly bent.

(When advancing either foot may be in front.)

The Body.—The body should be leaning slightly forward adopting a threatening attitude. The left elbow should be slightly bent and the point of the bayonet about the height of the chest, barrel slightly inclined to left, butt close into the hip, supported along the lower edge of the right forearm.

Rest Position

This is an instructional position which is taken on the order " Rest " from the " On Guard " position. To be used while explanations and demonstrations are being given.

The legs are straightened and the butt of the rifle placed between the feet and the rifle held at the band with the right hand.

METHODS OF ATTACK
The Long Point

So called because the rifle is used in the position which gives the longest reach.

(a) *At the Halt.*—To carry out the movement from the " On Guard " position.

Punch the rifle out to the full extent of the left arm, at the same time bending the forward knee and thrusting the body forward to the limit of balance from the rear heel which should be raised.

The movement should be harmonized to culminate in a decisive stab as the bayonet penetrates the target.

To Withdraw.—Slip the left hand up to the nosecap, then jerk the rifle back hard until the left forearm stops in the pit of the stomach ; at the same time sink back hard on the rear heel.

The rifle must be withdrawn on exactly the same line as it goes forward in making the point, otherwise it would be impossible to extract the bayonet from the opponent's flesh and clothing.

This must be done with a sharp movement or you may not extract your bayonet and will merely pull your opponent on top of you.

To Come on Guard.—Punch the rifle forward to the " On Guard " position.

(b) *At the Quick.* (In class formation or opposite dummy.)—This point is made exactly as taught " At the Halt," care being taken to see that the point enters the opponent's body at the same time as the advancing foot touches ground, thus ensuring that the weight of the body is behind the point.

To Withdraw. (From Dummy.)—As " At the Halt."

To Come on Guard.—The rifle is punched out as the rear foot advances, the left hand being slipped back to band at the same time.

NOTE.—The left hand is moved up to withdraw because it has been found that, when resistance is met by the point in actual practice against a dummy or body, the left arm bends, and to counteract this the left hand is moved forward to obtain full withdrawing leverage.

(c) *At the Charge.* (On Bayonet Range.)—Similarly to " At the Quick." The greatest care must be taken to make the point and stop the forward motion of body at correct distance from target, the natural tendency being to get too close before making the point.

The " Withdrawal " and " On Guard " positions are carried out as " At the Quick."

Dummy on Ground.

To Withdraw.—As for against hanging dummy, but to gain added leverage the left foot is placed on the dummy close to the bayonet at the same time as the left hand is slipped up the rifle.

The Short Point

This point is used when meeting another opponent as you are withdrawing from the first, and have not space or time to return " On Guard."

(a) *At the Halt.*—First order " Short Point Ready " at which the class will get to the " Long Point Withdraw " position by slipping the left hand forward and then pulling the rifle back till the left forearm meets the stomach.

The point is made as for a " Long Point."

To Withdraw.—Being so close up to your opponent it will be impossible to withdraw with the right hand below the small ; consequently the right hand is shifted to the point of balance to obtain greater leverage.

The " Withdraw " is then made as before.

NOTE.—In " Withdrawing " care must be taken that the rifle is kept in the same line as it went forward as it is now Butt heavy.

To Come on Guard.—Punch the rifle out with the left hand, at the same time bring the right hand back to the notch below the small. The left hand is then slipped back to the band.

(b) *At the Quick or Double.*—First make a Long Point and withdraw (left hand up), make the advancing point and withdraw as above.

The Jab

This point is made after withdrawing from a Short Point when you find another opponent close on top of you.

It is also made when you are suddenly confronted by an opponent whilst carrying the rifle in this position, *i.e.* in closely-wooded country, house clearing, or when it is not practical to carry the rifle in the normal on guard position.

The Jab is a short forward and upward stab, the object being to pierce your opponent's throat or face with the point. Withdraw is effected immediately so that, if the first blow is ineffective, it may be repeated, or possibly against another opponent within striking distance but against whom there is not sufficient time or space to return to the " On Guard " position and make a Long Point.

(a) *At the Halt.*—At the order " Jab Ready " the rifle is first brought to the " Short Point Withdraw " position, then the butt lowered slightly and the right hand shifted to the band ; at the same time both knees are bent slightly, the body assuming a crouching attitude.

To Come on Guard.—This is done in a similar fashion to returning " On Guard " from the " Withdraw " position of the Short Point.

(b) *At the Quick.*—First make a short point and withdraw, then make the jab, except that the rear foot is advanced. The whole movement is timed so that the jab is made with the point as the rear foot meets the ground.

This point may also be practised with a jump, *i.e.* the feet not crossed during this movement forward.

METHODS OF DEFENCE

The only method of defending oneself if unable to use the bullet or bayonet is a Parry. It is always made as a preliminary to a further attack.

Parries

A parry is a sharp blow in a forward and sideway direction on your opponent's rifle, and can be made from the following positions :—

(a) " *On Guard.*"—Punch the rifle forward to full extent of the left arm either to right or left, meeting your opponent's rifle as far away from your own body as possible.

The movement must never be wider than your own body, or you will not be able to follow on with a point immediately.

The parry must be short and crisp so that a point can be made immediately.

NOTE.—If armed with a long bayonet the parry to the left must be made with the back of the blade and to the right by the cutting edge.

(b) " *Short Point Ready.*"—Owing to the rifle being on the right side of body only a left parry is practicable. Carried out as above.

(c) " *Jab Ready.*"—The movement is made with a short chop forward with both hands to left or right with the cutting edge of long bayonet, returning automatically to the jab position to follow up with attack by jab.

The point should always be used if possible.

METHODS OF COUNTER ATTACK

Butt Stroke 1

This follows immediately on a Parry if unable to use the point.

(a) *At the Halt.*—First make a parry, then punch the butt of the rifle forward with the right hand so that the toe of the butt would strike an opponent in the fork, stomach or left forearm.

On completion, return on guard ready to finish off opponent with the point.

(b) *At the Quick.*—The movement is carried out as above, the rear foot coming forward at the same time as the butt stroke is made. The " On Guard " position is returned to immediately after making the stroke before advancing.

Butt Stroke 2

This is the immediate action after being parried by your opponent.

(a) *At the Halt.*—First adopt a position as if parried from a Long Point then, with a circular motion of both arms, the left hand moving downwards towards the left knee and the right arm moving upwards past the right ear, deliver a punch with the right arm to strike your opponent's face with the toe of the butt, keeping the left arm close to the thigh.

To Return on Guard.—Punch the left hand forward and pull the right hand to the " On Guard " position, care being taken to keep the point to the front.

(*b*) *At the Quick.*—As for " At the Halt " except that the rear foot advancing meets the ground at the same moment as the Butt arrives on the target.

RING AND BLOB STICK

This is used for working up speed and precision. The Ring being used as a target for the Point and the Blob end as a target for the Butt.

The Instructor will assume a somewhat threatening attitude when placing either end of the stick as a target for his pupil. The pupil will then make the requisite Point or Butt Stroke according to distance. The master works his pupil up by gradually increasing the number of points to be made consecutively. A good master will vary the use of his stick to make his pupil fight the target with speed and ferocity.

The stick can also be used to imitate a thrust with the opponent's bayonet making his pupil parry from any position and any distance.

The stick must be used intelligently so that it is made to represent real close quarters fighting and in this way can be of the utmost value in making a man proficient at handling his weapon and work up his fighting spirit.

Properly used, it can add great variety to the training, its great value lying in the necessity for men to act immediately on a visible indication instead of an order.

BAYONET RANGE

On completion and during all training the practical use of a range is of utmost importance to inculcate the dash required in a charge, and to produce the fitness required to make one.

The *very greatest attention* must be paid when on the range to the section *keeping in line*. The moral effect of bayonets in line is very much greater than a higgledy piggledy line and if the section is not in line it is impossible to use the bullet.

Obstacles must be overcome with dash. When surmounting a wall care must be taken that the body is not exposed to view on the top of the wall for more than a split second and never in an upright position.

The dress laid down in syllabus should be strictly adhered to.

Dummies.—These will be composed of fascines (bundles of brushwood some 8 in. in diameter and 2 ft. long, bound top and bottom, preferably with small wire rope), which are secured vertically and laterally in some form of gallows (*see* Appendix IV).

The reason for these fascines in lieu of the old-fashioned sacks is that :—

    (i) They provide definite resistance for making a point and withdrawing therefrom.

    (ii) Will last some 1000 per cent. longer.

Course.—Typical combined Obstacle Bayonet Course is shown in Appendix III.

USE OF BULLET

General Remarks

Having due regard to the conservation of ammunition, particularly in respect of R.Ms. landing from H.M. Ships, and in view of the difficulty of firing with any degree of accuracy from the hip, especially when moving at the " Double," no use will be made of the bullet on the move until within 20 to 15 yards of the enemy. From this distance onwards it may be advisable to fire a bullet. Such action enables the attacker to deliver an effective blow before getting close enough to kill with the bayonet.

Instruction in practical firing in this method will be given by the Small Arms Department. Preliminary instruction being undertaken during bayonet fighting periods as follows :—

(*a*) *At the Halt.*—Position of Rifle—from the " On Guard " position, straighten the left arm bringing the barrel uppermost, instead of slanting to the left, at the same time pushing forward the safety catch, and then gripping the Small of the Butt with the right hand, the index finger engaging the trigger, the eyes will be concentrated on to the target. The greatest care is to be taken that the Butt is pressed into the hip with the right hand and the angle of the barrel not being above the horizontal.

It must be particularly impressed that a miss high is certainly a waste of a round, whereas if low, there is more chance of hitting the next man or even a kill with a " rico." On the command " Bullet " from the Section Commander, the section will press the trigger, immediately working the bolt as for reloading.

(b) *At the Quick.*—The section will advance in quick time in the hip firing position, to get accustomed to this, and will fire and reload as already taught " At the Halt " on the command " Bullet."

(c) *At the Charge.*—The section will advance at the High Port and the " Double " (the idea can be conveyed here that the men are advancing through a smoke screen). On getting within distance (say, 50 yards) the Section Commander will give the order " Charge," when rifles will be brought to the hip firing position and the safety catch pressed forward with the forefinger. At 20 yards distance the Section Commander will give the order " Bullet," action thereon being taken as before. The target being then charged with the bayonet.

It is essential that the charge culminates with a point made on the ground, representing your enemy being finished off after being wounded in the guts, otherwise the spirit of the assault will be lost.

GENERAL NOTES ON BAYONET FIGHTING TRAINING

Reasons are given throughout for the method of training and for the use of each separate movement.

It must be impressed on all ranks that the training is designed to make the handling of the weapon automatic, particularly with the use of the Ring and Blob Stick.

Such commands in initial training as " Short Point Ready " and " Jab Ready " may appear somewhat unpractical when carried out " At the Halt," but it must be impressed that such positions can be of the greatest advantage under some conditions in street, house to house, trench or dugout fighting.   It may well be that the use of such positions will enable a man at a critical moment to save his own life and kill his enemy.

The whole training will, if properly conducted, undoubtedly give a man that confidence in his weapon which is so essential.

The practical application of the use of the Bullet at short range is the outcome of experience in house to house fighting.   Always remember that a Royal Marine may have to fight *any sort* of opponent at *any time* at *any place* in the world.

The following syllabuses of training are attached for general guidance:—

(i) Part I.   Elementary.

(ii) Part II.   Advanced.

PART I.—ELEMENTARY SYLLABUS

Lessons 2–6.—A general Revision will be given in every case at each period before the new Subject for that period is taught.

Lesson	*Subject*	*Remarks*
1.	Introductory Talk.	Explain general characteristics. Spirit of Bayonet, Vital parts of Body.
	High Port.	From Stand at Ease position.
	Class Formation.	2 ranks.
	On Guard Position.	From High Port and Rest positions.
2.	Long Point, at the Halt and at the Quick. (Instructors demonstrate.)	(*a*) Class formation. (*b*) Hanging dummies. (*c*) At Ring and Blob Stick.
3.	Two Long Points. (Instructors demonstrate.)	(*a*) Class formation. (*b*) Hanging dummies. (*c*) Ring and Blob Stick.
4.	Long Point (at Ground Dummy). (Instructors demonstrate.)	Foot and Hand to withdraw.
5.	Two Long Points. (Lessons 3 and 4.) (Instructors demonstrate.)	At ground, and hanging Dummy both at the Quick.
6.	Simple Assault Course Run.	(*a*) Slow time. (*b*) All out. Bring out Spirit of Bayonet and introduce use of Bullet, and give occasional " Fire " Order.

N.B.—**Dress.**—Lessons 1–5 will be carried out in Loose Order Steel Helmets and Respirators.

Lesson 6 will be carried out in Drill Order Steel Helmets and Respirators.

Occasionally respirators will be worn during B.T. practice.

PART II.—ADVANCED SYLLABUS

Lessons 7–13.—A general Revision will be given in every case at each period before the new Subject for that period is taught.

Lesson	*Subject*	*Remarks*
7.	Short Point.	(a) At the Halt and at the Quick class formation. (b) At Dummies. (c) Ring and Blob Stick.
8.	Jab Point.	(a) At the Halt and at the Quick. (b) At Dummies. (c) Ring and Blob Stick.
9.	Parries—From " On Guard," " Short Point Ready " and " Jab " positions. (Instructors demonstrate.)	(a) Parry left. Parry right. (b) Followed by point at the Halt and at the Quick.
10.	Full Assault Course. (Instructors demonstrate whole Course.)	Combine Assault with Obstacle Course. Occasional " Fire " order and Use of Bullet.
11.	Butt Stroke 1. (Instructors demonstrate.)	(a) With Ring and Blob Stick after having parried Right or Left. (b) Class formation.
12.	Butt Stroke 2. (Instructors demonstrate.)	(a) With Ring and Blob Stick after having been parried. (b) Class formation.
13.	Combination of (a) points, (b) points and butt strokes, (c) parries and points, (d) parries and butt strokes.	(a) Class formation. (b) At Dummies. (c) Ring and Blob Stick.

N.B.—**Dress.**—Lessons 7, 8 and 9 will be carried out in Drill Order Steel Helmets and Respirators.

Lessons 10, 11, 12 and 13 will be carried out in Fighting Order. Respirators will frequently be worn during these lessons until men can complete a full assault course with the respirator on.

APPENDIX I

CLASS FORMATION

APPENDIX II
BAYONET TRAINING STICK

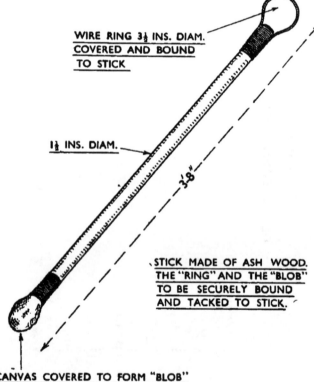

WIRE RING 3½ INS. DIAM. COVERED AND BOUND TO STICK

1⅛ INS. DIAM.

3'8"

STICK MADE OF ASH WOOD. THE "RING" AND THE "BLOB" TO BE SECURELY BOUND AND TACKED TO STICK.

CANVAS COVERED TO FORM "BLOB"

APPENDIX III

OBSTACLE AND BAYONET ASSAULT COURSE

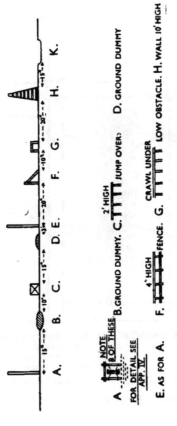

A.   B.   C.   D. E.   F.   G.   H.   K.

NOTE.
A. B OF THESE. B. GROUND DUMMY. C. JUMP OVER> 2' HIGH D. GROUND DUMMY
FOR DETAIL SEE APP. IV

E. AS FOR A.   F. FENCE. 4' HIGH   G. CRAWL UNDER LOW OBSTACLE. H. WALL 10' HIGH

K. WATER JUMP 6'6" WIDE

APPENDIX IV

HANGING DUMMY

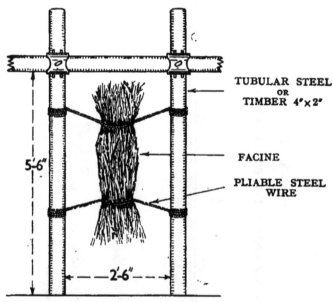

TUBULAR STEEL
OR
TIMBER 4″ × 2″

FACINE

PLIABLE STEEL
WIRE

5′-6″

2′-6″

FACINES SHOULD (1) PREFERABLY BE MADE OF BIRCH FOR DURABILITY.
(2) BE BOUND VERY TIGHTLY.
(3) HAVE A CORE OF THICKER TWIGS.

GROUND DUMMIES.   SIMILAR FACINES SHOULD BE USED.

NOTE.—Railway sleepers, cut to the correct size, may be used instead of facines.

CLOSE COMBAT

INTRODUCTION

The following is intended for the use of all officers and men, and is not merely for specialist instruction by qualified P. & R.T. Instructors.

Where the latter are available they are probably the best persons to take charge of initial training, but any officer or N.C.O. should be able to master the movements described herein and teach them to his men.

For the instruction of large bodies of men, a good way to introduce the subject is to either give a demonstration by experts or have a view of the Admiralty " Close Combat " film, showing the various movements in both slow and quick time.

The judicious and careful use of blank ammunition in pistol and rifle (Sections 9 (a), 9 (b) and 10) will be found most impressive and will contribute very largely in giving men confidence in the value of the method described.

In spite of the elaborate mechanization of modern warfare there often comes the time when it is man-to-man and hand-to-hand. Should you find yourself in such a situation there are many things you can do to defeat the enemy, even though you have no weapon and may appear to be at some disadvantage at first. These things are known as " Close Combat."

It has been found in training numbers of men in this subject, that if they are to retain their knowledge, it is *absolutely essential* that they *practise frequently* the movements themselves besides being shown them.

Particular care must be taken that the movements are carried out correctly as laid down in this handbook.

General Principles

Before going into details of method there are some general principles to be learned and remembered.

1. Forget all about the old British slogan of " Never kick a man when he is down." War is not a game, and there are no rules. You are up against a ruthless enemy who has been taught and trained to employ *every possible* means to blot you out. Remember, therefore, that it is your life or his, so do not hesitate to put him out of action as speedily as possible, regardless of the means employed.

2. Attack is the best defence, so be on the attack or ready for it at all times. In close combat the essentials of attack are—speed, determination, and ruthlessness.

3. An armed man will always have an advantage over an unarmed man, provided he thoroughly understands his weapon, but do not allow the fact that you are unarmed to disturb your confidence, because there are many ways in which you can get the better of the enemy in spite of his weapons.

4. If you find yourself disarmed and facing a man with a rifle or pistol you can be pretty sure that for some reason or another he does not wish to shoot—maybe he has no ammunition, or perhaps his weapon has jammed, or again he may not wish to make any noise—whatever the reason the fact that he does not shoot should give you confidence.

5. Always aim to get within arm's length of an armed opponent and then get closer still—the closer you are the less chance he has to use his weapons effectively.

6. Beware of tricks. Small grenades can be concealed in many places—on the shoulder, in the elbows, on the toes of boots, and so on. Remember the enemy is often prepared to blot himself out if he can take you with him, so if you have a gun shoot at the slightest sign—don't hesitate. If you haven't a gun don't take any risks—knock him out first and search him afterwards.

7. Finally, in Close Combat there is no such thing as defence—there is only attack or counter-attack. Your counter may contain a defensive movement, but only as part of your counter-attack.

METHODS

1. Blows and Where to Place Them

(a) *The Chin Jab.*—A sharp upward blow at the point of the chin with the heel of the hand. Keep the fingers spread and very slightly bent so that they may strike the opponent's eyes or nose. Use for chin only. A very effective blow if used with vigour and determination.

(b) *The Edge of Hand Blow.*—This may be more familiar to you as the " rabbit blow." Stretch the fingers of either hand and strike with the outer edge of the hand (*i.e.*, opposite to the thumb) at the back, sides or front of the neck.

NOTE.—Edge of the hand blows and chin jabs may be practised if the class is arranged in pairs and one man delivers the blow at the palms of the hands of his opposite number. For this purpose the hands of one man are raised, palm downwards, about in line with the face whilst the other uses them as targets.

Knee blows should always be used in conjunction with chin jabs.

(c) *The Shin Stamp.*—Scrape the outer edge of either boot sharply down either of your opponent's shins, finishing up with a vigorous stamp on his instep. If he is not wearing a top boot, a scrape on his shin will be most painful, but the stamp on his instep is the most important part of the blow and will be very effective, even though he is wearing a heavy rubber or leather top boot.

(d) *The Knee Blow.*—Raise either knee sharply into the opponent's fork or stomach.

(e) *The Kick.*—An ordinary powerful kick aimed at the fork, pit of the stomach, shin, kidneys, or face. Except in special situations, which will be described later, it is better not to use the kick until you have your opponent at a disadvantage or he is on the ground—a standing opponent who is on the alert will have no difficulty in countering your kick. If, however, you have been able to shake your opponent with a grenade, a kick will probably be found to be the best method of dealing with him while he is still suffering from shock, even though he may be still on his feet.

(f) *The Boxing Punch.*—The ordinary boxing punch aimed at the throat, the groin, the pit of the stomach or the kidneys. Don't use it at the chin—the chin jab is far more effective.

(g) *The Helmet Blow.*—Normally, you should never remove your helmet except under the conditions described hereafter in Section 4 (c), but if for any reason you have removed your helmet it can be a very useful weapon. Grasp it firmly with the thumb over the brim and the fingers inside and strike with the edge at the back or sides of the neck, or if your opponent is lying on his face, at the base of the spine.

2. The Cosh

This is, in effect, a truncheon. It may be made of wood or metal, or, better still, a length of flexible electric cable about 15–18 ins. long and 1–1½ ins. in diameter. It is a good thing to fit your cosh with a loop at the handle end so that you can loop it over your wrist. You can then have your hand free for use, but a quick swing upward will bring the cosh ready into your hand.

The best points to aim at with a cosh are the front, sides and back of the neck, the point of the shoulder, the groin, inside the leg just above the knee, the base of the spine or the shin.

When using the cosh do not strike straight downwards on top of your opponent's helmet. Strike downwards and inwards at the neck in the angle of head and shoulder.

3. Breakfalls

Before attempting to practise any of the following, it is necessary for all pupils to have a knowledge of the general principles of how to fall. If possible, breakfalls should be practised on mats, but they can be conveniently practised on grassland.

General Principles of Breakfalls

(1) When thrown try to meet the ground with as large a " breakfall " surface of the body as possible at the moment of impact.

(2) Avoid falling on any one point, i.e., shoulder, elbow or seat, etc.

(3) Keep the head off the floor during a fall.

(4) The shock or jar of a fall is taken with the arms or feet, and in some cases, both arms and feet are used simultaneously.

(5) When using one or both arms to break a fall, the main thing to remember is to deliver a sharp vigorous blow with the outstretched arm on the mat, from palm to shoulder, a fraction of a second before the body arrives. Thus the greater part of the shock is taken with the arms, with the result that the body reaches the ground comparatively lightly and without shock or jar.

. (6) The feet are brought into play in various falls, the fall being taken in this case with the soles of the feet assisted by the arms.

(7) The body should be kept loose and supple during a fall, only being braced at the actual moment of impact.

(8) Breakfalls should be practised at the commencement of every lesson, as they can always be improved and are never perfect. Throws should be practised slowly at first, gradually increasing in quickness. The speed of the throw must be determined, however, by the ability of the man being thrown to break his fall.

(9) In the early stages of practice and until at least a fair amount of proficiency has been attained in Breakfall, it is advisable for pupils to assist each other by easing one another to the mat when throwing.

1st Breakfall Exercise. (Lying on the back, with the arms loosely lying across the body and the knees bent.)

Roll to the right (1) and breakfall with the right (1) arm by swinging it smartly over the right (1) ; the arm should be straight and the fleshy part of the whole length of the arm should strike the mat at an angle of 45 degrees with the body; the eyes should be directed towards the knees, and the head kept off the mat.

2nd Breakfall Exercise. (Lying on the back, with the arms hanging loosely across the body and the knees bent.)

Raise the shoulders slightly off the mat, then fall back, and just before the shoulders meet the mat swing both arms outwards. The arms, as before, should be straight, and the fleshy part of the whole length of the arms should strike the mat at an angle of 45 degrees with the body an instant before the shoulders meet the mat; the eyes should be directed towards the knees, the head kept off the mat, and the seat clear of the ground.

3rd Breakfall Exercise. (Lying on the back, with the arms hanging loosely across the body and the knees bent.)

Strike the mat with alternate feet. The ankle should be stretched when striking the mat, so that you strike the mat with the sole of the foot and not with the heel only ; the eyes should be directed towards the knees and the head kept off the mat.

4th Breakfall Exercise. (Lying on the back, with the arms hanging loosely across the body and the knees bent.)

Strike the mat with both feet ; the ankles should be stretched when striking the mat, so that you strike the mat with the soles of the feet and not with the heels only : the eyes should be directed towards the knees, the head kept off the mat and the seat clear of the ground.

5th *Breakfall Exercise.* (Lying on the back, with the arms hanging loosely across the body and the knees bent.)

Strike the mat with the left (r.) arm and right (l.) foot at the same moment (as in 1st and 3rd Breakfall Exercises) and *vice versa*.

6th *Breakfall Exercise.* (Lying on the back, with the arms hanging loosely across the body and the knees bent.)

Strike the mat with both arms and feet at the same time (as in 2nd and 4th Breakfall Exercises).

7th *Breakfall Exercise.* (Standing.)

From the standing position fall forward, keeping the body straight but not rigid, and meet the ground with the fleshy part of both forearms.

8th *Breakfall Exercise.* (Standing.)

This should be practised in pairs. The men doing the exercise bend both knees as far as possible, the assistant then places his hands underneath both knees and with an upward and forward movement pushes the pupil on to his back, who should breakfall as in Exercise No. 6.

4. How to Attack a Man from behind when you are Unarmed

If you wish to take your opponent unawares, your approach must depend on the nature of the ground. You can only creep up slowly and silently over soft earth or sand—over gravel or debris you will have to make a rush for it and rely on getting at your opponent before he has time to turn.

As soon as you are close behind him, quickly swing one arm round his neck, bringing the forearm sharply against his throat. As soon as your arm contacts his throat, strike a knee blow at his back with the *opposite* knee (*i.e.*, left arm, right knee), at the same time clap your free hand over his mouth. This will cause him to fall backwards and you can then attack him with any kicks or blows previously described.

If your enemy should start to turn before you are close enough to attack him in the above manner, the only thing to do is to dive for his knee and tackle him low as in Rugby football. Launch yourself at the back or side of his legs aiming to hit him with your shoulder about six inches above the knees. Turn your head slightly to the left so as to avoid his rifle, as your shoulder strikes, fling your arms round his legs and hold them firmly. He is bound to come down and you can then pounce on him and apply blows or kicks.

When the nature of the ground permits a silent approach and you can get right up to your opponent without being heard, approach on all fours, and when within reach grasp him firmly below the knees with both arms (as for Rugby tackle), place your right shoulder above the knees and with a vigorous thrust of the shoulder and a pull with the arms, throw him on his face. As he falls retain the grasp of his ankles with both arms and kick to fork. This method is particularly suitable for a small man when attacking a person much bigger than himself.

5. What to do if you are Unarmed and Held Up by an Enemy with Rifle and Bayonet.

Remember that he is either unwilling or unable to shoot. He will almost certainly come towards you with his rifle fixed firmly in line with your body. Go towards him if you can—this will in itself put him off a bit—and when you are ready for your attack, fling something in his face. Anything will do, a clod of earth, a stone, a handful of gravel, a clip of ammunition, even a packet of papers or a notebook. Whatever it is it will make him blink, and distract his attention for just a fraction of time, and in that split second you must jump in and get inside his bayonet point and so to close quarters. As you go in you *must* parry his rifle and bayonet sharply to your left with a downward and outward movement of the left hand—on no account parry it in such a way as to bring the rifle between you and your opponent. Don't go for the weapon—go for the man, strike an edge of hand blow at neck or throat, or apply the chin jab and then follow up with other kicks or blows.

6. What to do if you are Unarmed and are Attacked by—

(a) *An enemy with a Rifle and Bayonet.*—When attacked, parry with the palm of your right hand and forearm on the back edge of your opponent's bayonet towards your left. Then quickly seize your opponent's left hand with both of your own and bind it tightly to the rifle. Twist the rifle sharply to the right, turning your back towards him as you do so, and extend your right leg outside his. Unfix opponent's bayonet and jab to face with left hand, maintaining grip of rifle with right hand.

(b) *An enemy with a Rifle and Bayonet.*—Parry in the same method as above, then seize the rifle with the left hand from underneath and just in front of your opponent's left hand and with your right hand on the butt behind your opponent's right hand. With a circular motion with both arms started by pulling hard with the right hand and pushing with the left, twist the rifle out of opponent's hands, and kill him with his own bayonet.

NOTE.—The above methods are introduced in order that each man may select the one best adapted to his own capabilities. Undoubtedly (b) is the better of the two, but is more difficult to perform. Again, there are occasions when (a) would perhaps be better than (b), depending on the attitude of the opponent.

(c) *An Enemy with a Pistol.*—Again, remember he is either unwilling or unable to shoot, but you *must* get to close quarters. Either approach him or, if he won't allow that, try and encourage him to come to you. By raising your arms or other similar movements indicating surrender you must persuade him to approach you until his pistol is only a few inches from your body. Then speak to him to distract his attention for a fraction of time, keeping your eyes fixed on his eyes. At the same moment swing your body sharply round on the hips and at the same time bring the nearest hand down in a sharp blow at his pistol or pistol hand, knocking it outwards. If his pistol is in his right hand your swing should be to *your right*, and the left arm used to strike at the weapon. The moment you have struck the weapon clear you swing back, using the chin jab, boxing punch at throat or to stomach, or perhaps better still a knee blow. Then go for his pistol and apply other blows or kicks as convenient.

(d) *An Enemy with a Knife or Bayonet.*—If you can get it off in time your helmet can be used as a shield and you must then wait your chance to rush in for a blow.

If he comes at you with the knife firmly in one hand ready for an *upward* thrust and you have had no time to get your helmet off, wait for him with a slight forward crouch and both arms ready for instant action, particularly the arm opposite to his knife hand.

As he strikes upward, strike downwards and outwards at his knife forearm with your own forearm and edge of hand, and at the same time removing your target by pushing the seat to the rear lunge forward and punch with your other hand for his stomach or chin jab if his face is thrust forward, as it probably will be. Follow up at once with further blows or kicks.

If he is wise he will probably approach you in a crouch position with both hands in front of him, passing the knife from hand to hand to put you off. This is one occasion on which you can use a kick at a man on his feet—kick at his fork, stomach or face, and follow up immediately with other kicks and blows.

If opportunity serves, you can again make use of the trick of throwing something at his face to distract his attention.

If your enemy is unwise enough to strike at you with a downward blow, proceed as in the next paragraph (*e*).

(*e*) *An Enemy with a Cosh.*—He has got to get within arm's length of you. As his arm comes downward in strike, crouch well down and parry the blow with the fleshy part of the left (right) forearm, fingers extended and the arm well bent. The head must be kept well down behind the forearm, the right hand ready to deliver a chin jab. Then follow up with either kicks or blows. Follow on your jump with a punch at his fork or stomach with the other hand, or a chin jab at his face if his head is thrust forward, as it probably will be.

7. (*a*) *An Unarmed Enemy comes at you with a Kick.*—As he kicks turn sharply left or right so as to bring you on the *outside* of and *facing* his kicking leg. At the same time lean slightly sideways towards him and sweep the near arm under his leg and then violently upwards, taking his leg too. He must go over backwards and, if your upward sweep is strong enough, the first part of him to hit the ground will probably be the back of his head. You have only to follow on and use one of the kicks or knock-out blows already described.

An alternative method which can be used, if you see the kick coming in time, is to turn your body to one side, at the same time raising the near foot so that the outer edge of your boot meets the kicking shin.

NOTE.—Your turn must be inwards from the kicking foot, *i.e.* right foot kick turn right and meet it with the left boot. This movement required very accurate timing and you must be ready to follow it up at once by jumping in for a blow or kick.

(*b*) *An Unarmed Enemy comes at you and then thinks better of it and turns to run.*—Jump after him and apply the Rugger tackle already described in para. 4.

(*c*) *Unarmed Enemy who attacks with kick whilst you are on the ground.*—You may be thrown to the ground during a struggle and your opponent may rush in to administer the *coup de grace* with his feet. As he comes in turn swiftly on to the side, at the same time drawing the lower leg well up beneath you and extending the upper one so that the kicker's shin comes hard up against the edge of your boot. Your hands should already be conveniently placed for a quick recovery, and you can take advantage of his discomfiture to step in and finish him off.

8. How to Release Yourself if—

(a) *Held round the Body from behind outside or inside the Arms.*—If wearing a helmet, jerk the head back sharply and try to strike the enemy in the face with the edge of your helmet.

At the same time claim one of his arms firmly with both hands and clasp it tight against your body. At the same time place your corresponding leg (*i.e.* if claiming right arm then use your right leg) outwards and backwards so that it is outside but as close as possible to your opponent's leg. Then turn your body sharply away from the extended leg, maintaining the grasp with your hands. The opponent will be thrown to the ground across your extended leg and you can then proceed to immobilise him.

(b) *Seized by the Neck from behind with Fingers.*—Immediately the fingers are felt round the throat, turn vigorously in either direction towards your opponent, particular effort being applied to the twist of the head. This movement, carried out with sufficient vigour as soon as you are gripped, will break his hold. The twist of the body will place you in an excellent position to deliver a knee blow which you may follow up with other kicks and blows.

(c) *Seized by the Neck from behind with Forearm at Throat.*—Grasp opponent's forearm with both hands, at the same time drop on the knee corresponding to opponent's forearm (*i.e.*, right forearm—right knee), and bend sharply forward towards the grounded knee. This will throw the enemy over your back or to one side of you. Jump on him and strike.

9. How to March a Prisoner

(a) *If you are Armed with Rifle and Bayonet.*—Make him raise his arms and—if possible—interlock his fingers at the back of his neck.

Keep your bayonet point about one yard clear astern of his back, and if he won't get on, don't on any account attempt to prod him on with the point—carry your rifle to the high port position and then kick him in the stern until he gets on. If he should make any move to turn or attack, bring your bayonet down with a slash at the angle of neck and shoulder.

If you carry your bayonet too close to him he has only to turn sharply and sweep it on one side—your shot will go wide by several feet.

(b) *If you are Armed with a Pistol.*—Make him put his arms as in (a). Keep your pistol about one yard clear astern of his back and if he won't get on, grasp his corresponding shoulder firmly with your free hand at the full extent of the arm (*i.e.*, left hand on left shoulder) and push him forward, keeping the pistol in the other hand well back ready to fire.

If you prod him in the back with your pistol he's got you cold. He has only to swing round and brush it to one side and he will be able to do this long before you can pull the trigger.

(c) *If you are Armed with a Cosh.*—Make him put his arms as in (a). Keep the cosh raised over your shoulder ready to strike and if he won't get on, grasp his corresponding shoulder firmly with your free hand at the full extent of the arm (*i.e.*, left hand on left shoulder) and push him forward, keeping the cosh well up and back in the other hand ready to strike. If you have to strike, do so downwards and inwards at the junction of neck and shoulder. Should the cosh glance off his helmet, head or shoulder, follow on immediately with a return blow in a horizontal direction at his shoulder or neck.

(d) *If you are Armed with a Knife.*—Proceed as for pistol, but in this case you *must* carry the knife with the thumb nearest the blade, and be ready to strike *upwards not downwards* at the small of the back under the ribs. If you strike downwards with a knife and miss, it's ten to one you will land in your own leg, and in any case it is not easy to strike a deadly blow with a knife downwards—you are almost certain to strike on a bone.

. (e) *If you have no Weapon handy.*—In this case you must knock your man out temporarily and then secure his hands behind his back in one of two ways :—

(i) Tie both thumbs closely together behind his back. Do not put the thumbs together and then tie them—secure your wire or twine on one thumb first and then make the other fast to it.

NOTE.—Only thin twine, cord or wire can be used—it is no good trying to tie thumbs with thick cord or rope. A strand of electric light flex or telephone cable will do admirably, but there should be a length of thin twine in your respirator haversack. If, when the thumbs have been secured, you have sufficient twine or wire to spare you can loop it round the man's neck and so draw his thumbs well up his back.

If you have nothing thin enough for a thumb tie you must use a belt or strap, and in this case tie his wrists as close as possible behind the back. Again, if you have sufficient spare end take a loop round the neck and draw the wrists close up.

(ii) If you have nothing to use as a strap and he is wearing a tunic or coat, undo the top buttons as necessary and pull the top portion of the tunic or coat down off his shoulders until it is level with a point just above his elbow.

Should you be unable to use either of the above two methods you can do only two things.

First, knock him senseless and keep him so until you can find a weapon of some kind.

Or, second, knock him about until you have got him into a state of complete submission, then grasp him firmly with one hand on the back of his collar and the other a good firm grip on the slack of the seat of his trousers. Push forward with the upper hand and pull upwards firmly with the lower one and propel him in front of you.

NOTE.—You can only afford to risk this method with a man who is thoroughly cowed because unless you remove his boots you are very vulnerable to a back kick and even if his boots are off he may get you with his heel in your fork or stomach.

Don't take any chances

10. What to do if you are being marched off as a prisoner

If you have studied Section 9 above carefully you can easily place yourself in enemy's position and see what to do.

If he has a rifle and bayonet, rifle only, pistol or knife, you must use all your wits to try and induce him to poke the weapon into your back and for obvious reasons you must have carefully noted beforehand in which hand or on which side he is carrying his weapon.

The moment you feel the weapon at your back swing round at full speed and sweep your near arm downwards and slightly outwards to strike his weapon arm clear of your body. Do not continue the arm sweep in an upward direction or you may only assist him to bring his weapon back on to your target.

SPECIAL NOTE.—Your turn should be *away* from his weapon side, *i.e.*, if he is carrying his weapon in his right hand your turn is to your left. Then jump in and hit.

If he is armed with a cosh you must entice him until he is close behind and then turn as before *but* this time instead of swinging the inner arm down keep it up. Duck away from his cosh arm and as he strikes, meet his forearm with the outer edge of your hand or forearm, at the same time punch hard to his fork or stomach. Follow with other blows or kicks.

11. How to hold a man down

If you have your enemy down and you want to keep him quiet for a while without tying him up, proceed as follows :—

Place your prisoner flat on his face, sit astride the small of his back facing his legs. Bend one of his legs backward from the knee and place the ankle behind his other knee; then bend the other leg back over the ankle and pull the foot firmly towards you. At the least sign of argument increase the pull on the foot—the harder you pull the quicker he will pack up.

12. Conclusion

You will see from the foregoing instructions that however desperate your situation may be, there is always a good chance of turning the tables on your enemy—of turning defeat into victory.

Don't forget to study your enemy's clothing and equipment before making up your mind what you are going to try to do—it may be that his rig will prevent you using certain blows—for instance, a German helmet protects the back of the neck but not the throat.

Learn the various movements carefully and then practise them slowly at first, working up later to full speed—speed is the key to success. It is a good thing to do your first practices in gym or sports rig, but later on as you become more expert you *must* practise in full battle equipment. Don't forget, too, that your opponent may be left-handed, and all movements should, therefore, be practised on both sides.

Finally, as Shakespeare says :—

" Be bloody, bold and resolute."

RECREATIONAL GAMES

(With Gear)

Game	Gear Required	Notes
Four - cornered Tug	Endless rope about six yards long. Four stones or canvas balls.	Four men hold rope in the form of a square and all pull against each other. Each man tries to get ball or stone placed about two yards from his corner.
Intercepting the Ball	Football ...	Class forms a large circle. One man gets in the centre and tries to touch ball as it is passed across or around the circle. If he succeeds the man who threw it goes to the centre and so on.
Blitz 'em ...	Football and watch	One team forms large circle, another team is grouped in this circle. Team outside throws ball and tries to hit team inside. When a player is hit he leaves circle. Team wins by shortest time taken to get opposing team out.
Mine Laying	Balls and Bucket or Stones and Steel Helmet.	Line teams up in single file about four yards apart. Place about four balls in front of team about two yards apart. The bucket is placed in front of No. 1. No. 1 collects balls one at a time and No. 2 places them back again one at a time and so on.

RECREATIONAL GAMES—*continued*

Game	Gear Required	Notes
Tunnel Ball	Football ...	Teams are lined up in a single file. Feet wide apart, about a pace between each man. The ball is passed from front to rear between the legs. When the rear man gets the ball he runs to the front of the team, whilst the whole team shift back one pace, and so on until No. 1 is in his original place. A similar game may be played by passing the ball over the head.
Ammunition Carrying. Relay	Buckets of sand or water or sandbags or boxes of ammunition	Line teams up in single file, with bucket in front of No. 1. On the word " Go " No. 1 runs about 25 yards and places bucket down and then runs back and touches No. 2, who runs and brings bucket back, and so on.
Charlie Chaplin Relay	Football, stick and glove	Teams line up as for most relays. No. 1 places ball between his knees, glove on his head and stick in his hand. On the word ." Go " he moves as quickly as possible, twirling the stick around, balancing the glove or object on his head and keeping the ball between his knees. (NOTE.—About 10 yards each way is far enough in this game.)

SUMMARY

The following schedule, which contains all the points dealt with in the syllabus, will be found useful in preparing a demonstration for instructional purposes, or as a guide for a series of lessons.

Introduction

Remarks and general principles, etc.

1. Breakfalls

2. Blows and Where to Place Them

(a) Chin jab.

(b) Edge of hand blow.

(c) Shin stamp.

(d) Knee blow.

(e) The kick.

(f) The boxing punch.

(g) The helmet blow.

3. The Cosh and How to Use It

4. How to Attack a Man from Behind when you are Unarmed

5. What to do if you are Unarmed, and are held up or attacked by—

(a) Enemy with rifle and bayonet.

(b) Enemy with pistol.

(c) Enemy with knife or bayonet.

(d) Enemy with cosh.

(e) Unarmed enemy who kicks.

(f) Unarmed enemy who kicks when you are on the ground.

6. **How to Release Yourself if—**
   (a) Held round the body from behind.
   (b) Seized by neck from behind.

7. **How to March a Prisoner if you are—**
   (a) Armed with rifle and bayonet.
   (b) Armed with pistol.
   (c) Armed with cosh.
   (d) Armed with knife.
   (e) Unarmed.

8. **What to do if you are being Marched Off as a Prisoner**

9. **How to Hold a Man Down**

RECREATIONAL GAMES—*continued*

FIELD GAMES

Game	Gear Required	Notes
Reveille Race	Fighting Order	An inter-sectional game. Section take off equipment, tunics boots, etc., and move to a poin about 50 yards away. On th word " Go " sections run to thei clothes, which have been dul mixed up and dress and fall ii as quickly as possible. Th time taken to fall in as a Sectio complete is taken, and points ar awarded for this, as well as ! o correctness of dress.
1. Tip and Run 2. Rounders ... 3. Handball ...	Bat and ball ... Bat or stick and ball Football ...	Too well known to requir description.
4. Away Sea Boats Crew	Poles or oars ...	Teams sit astride pole and ru backwards. Coxswain faces fo ward and guides crew aroun given point. Distance abou 20 yards each way.

NOTE.—In order to get personnel used to wearing a respirator, it : a good exercise to play these games wearing it.

RECREATIONAL GAMES—*continued*.

FIELD GAMES

Game	Gear Required	Notes
1. Stick Wrestling	Sticks 1 in. diameter, 18 ins. long	Wrestling carried out in pairs. Competitors standing opposite each other with the stick between them. One hand under grasp, one hand over grasp. Can be carried out with or without moving feet.
2. Ditto	Ditto	Competitors standing opposite each other. Sticks are held in a vertical position with one hand grasping the lower end of one stick and the upper end of the other. With the feet still try to take the sticks away from each other.

RECREATIONAL GAMES

Game	Gear Required	Notes
Convoy Running	One piece of gear per man	Four teams line up. Each man has one piece of gear. No. 1 collects all gear and runs forward 25 yards and places it in a heap. No. 2 then collects and distributes it to team. No. 3 as for No. 1.
Looting	Approx. six items per team	Circle or mat in each corner. One team in each corner. Team's gear placed in corner on mat. Object : To collect as much gear as you can.
Load the Gun.	Ball, Stick or Brick.	Four teams. Circle on ground. Instructor throws ball some distance from circle. Object : See which team can place ball in circle.
Climbing Relay	20-ft. tubular or pole.	Team carries tubular 25 yards. No. 1 climbs tubular, or team climb in turn. Finishing at start point.
All fours Hand Ball	Ball and Clubs	As for handball except that you must remain on all fours. Object : Knock down opponent's club.
Carrying wounded	Stout stick. Approx. 4ft.	Four teams. Nos. 1 and 2 use stick as chair to carry No. 3 25 yards. Then as for express trains.
Pentathlon. Log	250 lb. log, approx.	Four teams. (1) Roll log 25 yards. (2) Raise log vertical and horizontal alternately for 25 yards. (3) One of team climb to top of leg. Return to starting position.

RECREATIONAL GAMES—*continued*

Game	Gear Required	Notes
Pentathlon. Tubular	20-ft. tubular	Four teams. (1) Boat race for 25 yards. (2) One man climbs tubular. (3) Tubular passing between the legs. Return to starting position.
Pole wrestling	2 logs 250 lb. 2 mats coir	Four teams. Two teams to each log with log on shoulder facing one another with space in centre of log so that one man from each team can sit on log facing each other. Object : To knock each other off. Each man in team has a turn.
Treasure Hunt	Envelope. Stop watch	First team with items mentioned in sealed envelope. NOTE.—One item must call for a team effort. Used as first game you can supply all gear.
Land mines	Club	Each team in circle catching hold of hands. Club in centre. Object : To make someone knock the club over.

AGILITY EXERCISES

These exercises provide another form of variety in exercising the body, and are of considerable value in maintaining a man's suppleness and speed of movement.

If practised at fairly frequent intervals they will prevent a man becoming prematurely " Set."

The following is a selection of simple agility exercises which do not require a great amount of skill and should be easily performed by the average marine.

They are best carried out on mats, but can quite conveniently be performed on grassland.

1. Forward Roll—

    from (a) Crouch.

          (b) Standing.

2. Dive over low back or obstacle and forward roll.

3. Backward Roll—

    from (a) Crouch.

          (b) Standing.

4. Cartwheel.

5. Handstanding—

    (a) With assistance—in pairs. One man throws up and support catches his ankles assisting to maintain balance.

    (b) Against wall.

    (c) In pairs—Support lies down with knees raised. The other man, placing hands on support's knees and throwing up, being assisted at the shoulders by the hands of the support.

6. Head and hand balance.

BAYONET FENCING

Footwork

This is the most important part of training and should never be neglected. Exercise the following, first without, then with, the rifle.

1. The on guard position.
2. The advance.
3. The retire.
4. The lunge.
5. The advance by jump.
6. The retire by jump.
7. The pass forward.

Attacks

Quick simple attacks are much more successful in competitions than the more complicated ones, and are less liable to be defeated by the stop hit, such as :—

1. Direct point.
2. Point by disengage.
3. Throw point and pass forward.
4. High point.
5. One—two.

These attacks should first be practised at a pad fixed to a guard rail, wall or bulkhead to get perfect execution.

Defence

Impress the importance of a return point after parrying. Remember that practice in parrying is just as necessary as in attacking. Make the parrying movement short and crisp, and make it sufficiently far enough to the right or left to just clear your own target. This may be practised by one man attacking and the other defending, but it should be remembered at all times that both men should be wearing a complete set of Bayonet Fencing gear.

Fights

In the later stages of training arrange fights with other units, this will provide novices with the necessary experience of competitive conditions. Don't be too ambitious when arranging competitions, as a severe defeat in these competitions will have a bad moral effect on the inexperienced members of your team.

Dress

Have your team in a clean uniform dress: a smart and well turned out team has a great moral effect on your opponents. Khaki drill trousers are very comfortable to fight in.

Decisions

Never question the referee's decisions, accept defeat with good grace. Don't forget to shake hands with your opponent after the fight.

Arena

Measurements—a square having sides of 40 feet, and this may be marked out with whiting, chalk, stones, wood, etc., depending on conditions and material available.

Competitions

May be run as a team or pool. Teams may be of any odd number, but never more than 18 and a leader. In the event of a draw the leader fights off. Pools of eight may be run, but it is advisable to keep the number in a pool to six or less.

Each fight should consist of the best of five hits.

TUG-O'-WAR

Rules for Inter-Service Tug-o'-War are laid down in the Royal Naval Sports Handbook, published annually.

N.C. officers or men who have little knowledge of this subject are advised to confine their training to the following :—

(a) Preliminaries, i.e., lining out, boot inspection, taking up the rope, etc.

(b) Good position on the rope.

(c) Correct position of the feet.

(d) Perfect team work.

1. *First Practice.*—Practice slowly getting into position and correcting faults, then taking the strain quickly, and very short pull.

2. *Second Practice.*—Concentrate on pulling together, retaining ground gained. Continue to correct faults. Introduce half-minute pulls, all out.

3. *Third Practice.*—Practice checking opponents, heaving, and continue aiming at perfect timing in both the heave and check.

NOTE.—The position on the rope, the heave and the check have already been explained on page 55.

Advanced Training

If a long period of training is available, the lock can be practised, but it is to be emphatically noted that unless completely mastered the lock is of little value. Further, although the lock may be a rest for the team by a change of position, work on the rope must continue without the slightest pause, otherwise it will only result in failure.

TUG-O-WAR—*continued*

	Method	Remarks
The Lock	The rope runs across the upper part of thigh, and is bound in this position by pulling with the foremost arm, and pressing with the rear hand, which is about six inches behind the thigh.	Equal strain on both legs. Position must not be too low. The Lock must be taken without the opposing team seeing it. Best done from centre man outwards, or from rear to front.
Heaving in Lock	The seat is lowered as the forward arm pulls, the rear arm presses down and maximum pressure is made with feet and legs.	The movement generally is to downward and to the rear. Keep feet still until last moment and then move them quickly.
Checking in Lock	The rope is placed low by a general heavy pressure downwards as low as possible.	Must be done as a team together. Prepare for counter heave.
Coming out of Lock	Bring rear hand forward to normal heaving position and together pull through.	Must be a surprise movement and is best done on a signal. Back and leg must be used strongly.

At all times in the Lock—keep the rope lively.

HINTS ON TRAINING

1. Aim to get at least two training periods a day for one hour.

2. Try to get weights rigged up either aboard ship or ashore, and start your training on this, faults are more easily corrected this way.

3. Later, vary the weights with live pulling and change the training ground as much as possible. Introduce P.T. Exercises, Tubular Bar Work, Log Exercises, and frequent games and competitions into the training.

SCORE SHEETS FOR TEAM COMPETITIONS

Example team score card, eight and a leader :—

										Total Wins.
" A " Battery ...	W	W	L	W	W	L	W	I Leader.		5
Points against ...	. .	. .	. .	. .	. .	. .	. .			
	. .	. .	. .	. .	. .	. .	. .			
" B " Battery ...	L	L	W	L	L	W	L	W		3

Referee.....................................

Example pool sheet, five competitors :—

	Names.	Smith.	Jones.	Robinson.	Brown.	Holwell.			.
Names	Nos.	1	2	3	4	5			Total Wins
Smith	1		W	L	L	L			1
Jones	2	L		L	L	L			0
Robinson	3	W	W		W	W			4
Brown	4	W	W	L		L			2
Holwell	5	W	W	L	W				3

First place ... ... Robinson.
Second place ... ... Holwell.
Third place ... ... Brown.

Date.............................   ....Referee.

Order of Assaults

Five Competitors		Six Competitors				Seven Competitors				Eight Competitors					
1	4	1	4	4	5	1	4	1	3	1	5	3	5	7	8
2	3	2	5	1	2	2	5	4	6	2	6	4	6	1	3
4	5	3	6	3	5	3	6	2	7	3	7	1	8	2	4
1	2	1	5	4	6	1	7	3	5	4	8	2	5	5	7
3	5	2	6	1	3	4	5	1	6	1	6	3	6	6	8
2	4	3	4	2	4	2	3	2	4	2	7	4	7	1	4
1	5	1	6	5	6	6	7	3	7	3	8	1	2	2	3
3	4	2	3			1	5	5	6	4	5	3	4	5	8
2	5					3	4	1	2	1	7	5	6	6	7
1	3					2	6	4	7	2	8				
						5	7								

KNOCK-OUT COMPETITION
METHOD OF MAKING A DRAW

The following method will be found most useful in running all forms of K.O. competitions, *e.g.*, Inter-Platoon Football Competitions five Platoons, the welter weight Boxing Competition with 9 entries, etc., etc.

Rule.—Subtract the number of entries from the number above it having a power of 2. *i.e.* :—

5 entries 8–5 therefore there are 3 byes.

9 entries 16–9 therefore there are 7 byes.

Draw.—9 entries.

```
A bye   A ⎫
B  ,,   B ⎬ ......B ⎫
C  ,,   C ⎫          ⎬ ......B ⎫
D  ,,   D ⎬ ......D ⎭          ⎬ ......B   Winner
E  ,,   E ⎫ ......F ⎫          ⎭
F  ,,   F ⎭          ⎬ ......F ⎭
G  ,,   G ⎫ ......I ⎭
H  ⎫           
I  ⎭ ......I ⎭
```

(21936) 44616/P.7412 10,000 4/45 K.H.K. Gp. 8/8 TS.13757

9 781783 313778